Exalting
THE NAMES OF
JESUS

Exalting
THE NAMES OF
JESUS

WILLIAM D. WATLEY

Judson Press
Valley Forge

Exalting the Names of Jesus

© 2002 by Judson Press, Valley Forge, PA 19482-0851
All rights reserved.

Unless otherwise indicated, Bible quotations in this volume are from the New Revised Standard Version, copyright © 1989 by the Division of Christian Education of the National Council of the Churches of Christ in the United States of America. Used by permission. All rights reserved.

Bible quotations marked KJV are from the *Holy Bible,* King James Version.

Library of Congress Cataloging-in-Publication Data

Watley, William D.
      Exalting the names of Jesus / William D. Watley.
      p. cm.
ISBN 0-8170-1431-4 (pbk. : alk. paper)
      1. Jesus Christ—Name. I. Title.

BT590.N2 W25 2002
232—dc21   2002020526

Printed in the U.S.A.

08 07 06 05 04 03 02

10 9 8 7 6 5 4 3 2 1

✗✗ CONTENTS ✗✗

✕✕ PREFACE ✕✕

WHEN WE CONSIDER THE IMPACT AND THE IMPORT OF the Lord Jesus Christ in history and the devotion that he engenders in the lives of we who follow and love him, we are not surprised to find a number of names and descriptions of him in Scripture. I am grateful for the privilege of presenting this book on some of the biblical names by which our Lord is called, worshiped, adored, and followed.

As in my previous works, a number of persons have assisted in the production of this book. I am again grateful to my beloved sister and friend Mrs. Carolyn Scavella, who has served as the primary reader and editor for this work. Down through the years her editorial contributions to my writing have been immeasurable. This work is no exception. I am also grateful to my executive minister and young colleague at St. James A.M.E. Church, Rev. Raquel St. Clair, for her assistance in editing and for her valuable insights. The Christian church will be hearing much from this young, scholarly, and anointed woman of God. I am also grateful to our church administrator, Mrs. Delores Johnson, who coordinated the efforts of our secretarial staff, especially those of Mrs. Sherri Henderson and Ms. Mia Richardson, who typed the manuscript. A special word of commendation goes to my personal assistant and secretary, Rev. Ingrid Gales, for all that she did in preparing the manuscript, as well as for keeping up with my usual, hectic schedule.

I am grateful for the people of St. James A.M.E. Church in the city of Newark, New Jersey, who continue to be a receptive and encouraging flock in my efforts to preach God's Word. I am grateful to my wife, Mrs. Muriel Watley, who continues to pray me through my various visions and projects and who puts up with my wired and erratic writing schedule without complaint. I am grateful for her own faith walk with the Lord.

Since my last publication, I have been blessed with the birth of my first grandchild. (Note the possessive terms "I" and "my" to the exclusion of the other grandparents and great-grandparents!) My daughter and son-in-law, Jennifer and Charles Maxell, have blessed our family with an adorable baby girl, full of joy and Spirit/spirit, with intelligence bordering on genius. I am pleased to dedicate this book to our granddaughter, *Madison Savannah Maxell*. My prayer is that, as God moves in her life, she will know Jesus for herself in the fullness of the various names by which he is known, worshiped, affirmed, loved, and followed.

William D. Watley, Ph.D.
Fall 2001

Lion and Lamb

Revelation 5:1-6

*"See, the Lion of the tribe of Judah,
the Root of David, has conquered, so that
he can open the scroll and its seven seals."
Then I saw between the throne and the four
living creatures and among the elders a Lamb
standing as if it had been slaughtered....*
(Revelation 5:5-6)

IN THIS PASSAGE OF SCRIPTURE, JESUS THE CHRIST, THE risen and exalted Lord, is described as both Lion and Lamb. When someone was needed to open the great scroll of heaven and a search party was sent out to cover the pages of history, to examine the lives of those who were presently alive, and to peek even into the potential of generations unborn, no one was found worthy. John the Revelator began to weep because it seemed that the mysteries of heaven's great scroll would be forever sealed and unrevealed. However, one of the twenty-four praise elders seated around God's throne told him not to weep because the Lion of the tribe of Judah, the root of David, had conquered everything necessary in order to open the scroll. The Lion had conquered sin and had conquered death, for heaven's mysteries are revealed only to those with enough faith and fortitude to conquer the temptations, trials, and tragedies of life. Drying his eyes, John looked up and expected to see this mighty lion but instead saw a slain lamb.

Jesus as Lion and Lamb means that he has more than one way of approaching us and addressing our situation. When we have sinned and fallen short of God's glory, we don't need a lion of condemnation and judgment attacking us and ravaging our spirit. When we are already feeling like a nobody, we don't need a stern lion beating us up and making us feel worse. We need a gentle word from the Lord. We need a word of comfort and encouragement. We need the Lamb to speak tenderly and tell us, "Come to me, all you that are weary and are carrying heavy burdens, and I will give you rest" (Matthew 11:28). Justice says that we deserve a lion to slay us, but mercy says, "I'm going to send a lamb and let you know that you have another chance."

But, when we get comfortable with being miserable; when we start feeling so sorry for ourselves and are tempted to stay down; when we've been down so long that getting up doesn't even cross our minds (or if it does, it seems like an impossibility), then we don't need a lamb comforting us in our misery. We need the Lion with power to pull us up. We need the Lion with power to command us to take up our bed—to take up those things we've been clinging to and resting upon—and walk. Sometimes we need a lamb and sometimes we need a lion. That's why Jesus is so special. He's both Lion and Lamb and is able to be just what we need him to be.

When I heard the words *lion* and *lamb,* what struck me first was how different those creatures are. Their personalities are so different. Jesus as Lion and Lamb covers the whole of our personalities, our divergence and contradictions. The Jesus who is Lion and Lamb relates to the Peter in us that is devoted to him and understands the Peter in us that denies him. He understands the Paul in us that is a hell-raiser and relates to the Paul in us that is a heaven-proclaimer. He relates to the Thomas in us that is willing to follow him to Jerusalem but understands the Thomas in us that still questions and doubts. He understands the James and John in us that are ambitious and self-centered and relates to the James and John in us that are beloved and giving. As Lion and Lamb, Jesus understands our weaknesses but relates to our strength, and he loves us with all our contradictions.

When we think of the lamb, we think of green pastures, but when we think of the lion, we think of wild jungles. As Lamb, Jesus is able to give us peace when our spirits become overly anxious and fretful. As Lamb, he says, "Consider the lilies of the field, how they grow; they neither toil nor spin, yet I tell you, even Solomon in all his glory was not clothed like one of these" (Matthew 6:28-29). But, as Lion, he walks with us through the wild, untamed places of life. As Lion he says, "In the world you face persecution. But take courage; I have conquered the world!" (John 16:33). As Lion and Lamb he combines both green-pastures peace and wild-jungle survival.

In other words, when Jesus Christ is in your life as Lion and Lamb, he can give you peace in your spirit and peace in your mind, even as you live amidst the wild, untamed places and people of life. Bills may threaten to consume. Ferocious beasts on the job, in the home, in the neighborhood, and in the church may be ready to pounce on you, but if you know in whom you have believed and are persuaded that he is able to keep all that you have committed to him, then you can lie down and sleep in peace. You can wake up in the morning with praise, walk around with a smile, and hold your head up in confidence. Even though you live in a jungle, you can carry green pastures in your spirit.

Another difference between lions and lambs: Lambs eat in the day and sleep mostly at night; lions tend to be nocturnal creatures that sleep a lot during the day and become very active at night. Jesus as Lion and Lamb assures us that we have twenty-four-hour protection. Whether we are in a noontime of song or the midnight of sorrow, he's awake. Whether enemies are working in the day or plotting at night, he's awake. He has around-the-clock presence and around-the-clock power. He transformed Legion with his demons in the day; he himself was transfigured at night. He fed the five thousand during the day, but he walked on water at night. He called Lazarus from the grave during the day, but he arose from the grave while it was still dark. As Lion and Lamb, Jesus assures us that we are always covered.

Most of all, as Lion and Lamb, Jesus the Christ is our perfect deliverer. As Lamb, he is the sacrifice for our sins; as Lion, he proves his strength over the grave. As Lamb, he

4

endures the stripes inflicted by human enmity; as Lion, he demonstrates the stamina of heavenly endurance. As Lamb, he shows the gentleness of his grace; as Lion, he shoulders the greatness of his glory. As Lamb, he models obedience; as Lion, he manifests omniscience. As Lamb, he accepts lowliness; as Lion, he ascends to the loftiness of heaven. As Lamb, he sheds his blood; as Lion, he achieves our breakthrough. As Lamb, he is servant; as Lion, he is savior. As Lamb, he is killed; as Lion, he is king. As Lamb, he is rejected; as Lion, he is resurrected. As Lamb, he bears the cross; as Lion, he wears the crown.

Hail, Lion of Judah! Holy is the Lamb!

thank you Lord

✕ **2** ✕

The Wheel Within a Wheel

Ezekiel 1:15-16

As I looked at the living creatures,
I saw a wheel on the earth beside the
living creatures, one for each of the four
of them ... and the four had the same form,
their construction being something like
a wheel within a wheel. (Ezekiel 1:15-16)

THE WHEEL WITHIN A WHEEL IS ANOTHER OF THE GREAT symbols of Christ that those of us who have come up in the black church have heard about all our lives. Who among us is not familiar with the famous spiritual?

Ezekiel saw the wheel, way up in the middle of the air.
Ezekiel saw the wheel, way in the middle of the air.
The big wheel runs by faith,
the little wheel runs by the grace of God.
It's a wheel in the middle of a wheel,
way in the middle of the air.

Yet, as deeply embedded as this symbol is in the cultural theology of African Americans, most of us would be hard pressed to explain what we are talking about when we say Jesus is the "Wheel in the middle of the wheel," as the King James Version says. Most of us just say it, accept it, and go on from there.

Perhaps part of the difficulty in trying to explain the meaning of Jesus as the Wheel within a Wheel comes from the context in which the reference is found. Ezekiel's vision that describes the configuration of wheels is itself a very difficult passage to understand. I'm not sure anybody really understands all that Ezekiel was saying in this passage. I do know, however, that Ezekiel believed he was having a vision of God in the heavenly realm. If that is the case, we can understand the difficulty and the complexity of this passage. Some things are too great and too wonderful to be described by human language. As marvelous as language is and as many words as Webster's unabridged dictionary tells us that we have at our disposal, there are some experiences that are so awesome that when we try to explain them or put them into words, we find ourselves stumbling, faltering, and grasping for an expression that tells us how we feel.

How do we express love in words? How do we express in words what we feel when we behold a majestic sunset or hear a symphony of classical, jazz, or gospel music? How do we express in words what we feel when we make love to someone we truly love and who loves us back? We talk about our feelings, but when we finish we still feel that love is more unsaid than said. How do we describe in words our experience of the Holy Spirit? What does it feel like to be saved? What does it feel like to know that we are truly loved by God? We really can't express what we feel so we come up with words and phrases that are inadequate—but they are the best we can do, with the hope that somebody will get some glimmer of understanding of what we mean. We say things to describe our experience of God: "It's like fire shut up in my bones!" "Something hit me in the top of my head and ran on down to the soles of my feet!" "I felt joy bells ringing in my soul, a new melody in my heart and a new song of praise on my lips!" "I felt joy overwhelming, all glorious, victorious!" "I got peace that passes understanding."

In this passage in Ezekiel, the prophet is having a spiritual experience that includes a vision of what he believes to be the supernatural, and he is struggling to describe in normal human language what he is seeing. Part of his vision involves a configuration of wheels that are turned by wheels at their centers. I don't know the exact meaning of this vision, but let me suggest a couple possibilities.

The wheels that Ezekiel saw were constantly moving. Thus, I am reminded that God is always on the move. God is not some static being who sits high and looks low. When I'm in trouble I need somebody to do more than sit and look! God is spirit. The Hebrew word for "spirit" is *ruach* and the Greek word is *pneuma*. Both words mean "wind" and "breath." Wind and breath don't stand still; they are on the move.

This is one reason why Ezekiel sees God as turning wheels. He sees God on the move. I'm glad that God is spirit, wind, and breath because when we get into trouble, we need God to be on the move. When the devil begins to disrupt and corrupt, we *need* God to be on the move to counteract. When the Israelites reached the banks of the Red Sea, God's *ruach* was on the move: God's spirit blew a path of dry land through the watery deep. When the Israelites were in the wilderness without food, God was on the move: God's *ruach* blew quail in every evening and brought up manna every morning. When Jesus was hung high on Calvary and buried low in a borrowed tomb, God was on the move: God's *pneuma* raised him up on Sunday to stoop no more. When the believers gathered in the upper room to receive the promise from heaven on the day of Pentecost, God was on the move: God's *pneuma* came as the wind and filled the whole house.

God is constantly moving. God's work is constantly on the move because his promises are being fulfilled everyday. God's will is on the move because the kingdoms of this world *will* become the kingdom of his Christ and of our Lord. It was William Cowper who wrote, "His purposes will open fast, Unfolding every hour…. God moves in a mysterious way, His wonders to perform."

Ezekiel's vision of the wheels tells me about more than God's movement. Ezekiel noticed that in the midst of the turning wheels there was a centering, guiding wheel, and here is the image of Jesus, the centering Wheel within the turning Wheel of God's spirit. The insight gleaned from this name is the truth that Christ stands in the midst of all that God is doing. The writer of Hebrews tells us, "Long ago God spoke to our ancestors in many and various ways by the prophets, but in these last days he has spoken to us by a Son, whom he appointed heir of all things, through whom he also created the worlds" (Hebrews 1:1-2). As the Wheel within a Wheel, Jesus is the center of life. Peter declared, "You know that you were ransomed from the futile ways inherited from your ancestors, not with perishable things like silver or gold, but with the precious blood of Christ, like that of a lamb without defect or blemish" (1 Peter 1:18-19). The Samaritan woman told everybody, "Come see a man who told me everything I have ever done! He cannot be the Messiah, can he?" (John 4:29). The dying thief asked, "Jesus, remember me when you come into your kingdom" (Luke 23:42). Christ is the central access to heaven and life eternal.

Thus, when we say that Jesus is the Wheel within a Wheel, we are saying that, in the midst of all that God does, Jesus is the central, pivotal person. To have him in our lives, we must make Jesus our center. He cannot exist on the periphery or as an afterthought; he must be central to our existence, to our very being. Somebody said, "I woke up this morning with my mind stayed on Jesus"—our central, guiding Wheel.

The gospel artist Richard Smallwood has called Jesus "Center of My Joy." Our foreparents sang, "He keeps the prayer wheel turning. He keeps the fire burning. He keeps salvation coming. He keeps demons going. He keeps power flowing." Jesus, the Wheel within a Wheel, is our center who keeps us beloved and focused, in perfect peace because our minds are stayed on him.

✖ 3 ✖

Rose of Sharon

Song of Solomon 2:1

I am a rose of Sharon,
a lily of the valleys.
(Song of Solomon 2:1)

THROUGHOUT THE YEARS, THE ROSE OF SHARON HAS BEEN another messianic metaphor particularly popular in the traditional African American preaching idiom. Jesus as the Rose of Sharon reminds us of three great truths.

Sharon was a plain, an open stretch of land, in Palestine. In biblical times, anybody could travel there and gather up the abundance of roses and lilies that grew there. A rose from the plain of Sharon was not like the roses that grew in Solomon's garden, shut up within high walls, cultivated only to be touched, gazed upon, and enjoyed by an elite few. The roses of Sharon were available and accessible to everybody. Anybody could enjoy their beauty, smell their fragrance, or hold them in their hands. And so it is with Jesus, our Rose of

Sharon. He is accessible to everyone who will come to cherish the beauty and fragrance of his being.

There are those who want to box Jesus in or build a fence around him and say to everybody who does not see things according to their narrow perspective, "Unless you approach Jesus our way, unless you're baptized our way, unless you get him the way we got him, unless you receive the gifts that we have received, unless you dress in certain styles or look a certain way or have a certain background—only then can you have a share in him. Jesus is our private possession." We have all heard such claims: "Unless your church is a part of this denomination or that tradition or the other conviction" or "Only Prophet Self-Righteous or Bishop Know-It-All, Mother My-Way-or-No-Way or Brother Windbag Hypocrite has the last and final and true revelation. And only if you give him a piece of money or allow her to work some hoo-do, voo-do, and mo-jo on you, can you get into the throne room of *my* God."

That's not how you get to the Rose of Sharon. Jesus is not hidden behind some strange formula or esoteric doctrine that is accessible to only a few. You don't have to read any special Bibles, magazines, or newspapers to discover him. He's available to everybody. He simply says, "Whosoever will, let them come" (see Mark 8:34). If you need him all you have to do is call his name, *Jesus*. "Come unto me, all ye that labour and are heavy laden, and I will give you rest" (Matthew 11:28, KJV). You need no special incantation or phony formula, no crystal balls, no special readings. Just call his name, *Jesus*. No matter who you are or where you are, what you've done or where you've been—his grace is growing, his blood for cleansing is flowing, his delivering power is available all around you. Just reach out and touch him for yourself. And if you can't call his name, just wave your hand by faith; he will see you. And if you can't wave your hand or call his name aloud, just think *Jesus,* and he will come to you. Jesus, our Rose of Sharon, is available to you.

Jesus as Rose signifies more than his availability. As we all know, in our culture and day, the rose has become a symbol of love. Jesus Christ as Rose of Sharon is God's eternal reminder of how much we are loved. There are times when we can feel pretty lonely and even forsaken—when we can almost feel the breath of the hell hounds rapidly closing in, when things are going from bad to worse, when our prayers don't seem to be heard, when the breakthrough we have been looking for hasn't happened, and we begin to wonder if God indeed has forgotten about us. That's when we need to think about Jesus our Rose, whose coming was motivated by love, whose life reverberated with love, whose actions were driven by love, whose death was for the sake of love, whose resurrection was demanded by love, and whose second coming is the fulfillment of love's longing.

Nothing but love can explain why Jesus would choose to exchange heaven's glories for earth's shame and the praises of angels for the curses of men—nothing but love. Nothing can explain why Jesus would feel the touch from a single, bleeding woman in the midst of a jostling crowd or hear the cry of blind Bartimaeus above the noise of the masses—nothing but love. Nothing can explain why Jesus chose to hang on a cross and die for your sins and mine when he could have called ten thousand angels to destroy this world and set him free— nothing but love. There was no reason for him to rise and empower the very ones who had deserted and denied him in his dark hour—no reason but love. And now that he has returned to glory and is again seated at the right hand of God the Father, there is not one reason for Jesus to return a second time for those of us who are still on earth and who believe in his name—no reason but love. If some of us had been treated as Jesus was treated, once we got back to heaven we would wash our hands of earth. However, because Jesus our Rose loves us so much, not only did he promise the Holy Spirit who proceeds from the Father and the Son to keep and guide us, but he himself promised to come back for us with rewards for good and faithful service.

Thus, in times of loneliness and trouble, when we want to feel loved, think about Jesus. If we think about Moses, we might think about the righteousness of law that we fail to keep. If we think about Elijah, we might think of fire-and-brimstone religion and feel condemned by its stern judgment. If we think about Daniel, we might think of his prayer and fasting and wish we were as faithful as he was. If we think about Amos, we might think of social justice and be overwhelmed by all of life's complex social problems. But when we think about Jesus, our Rose, we think about how we are loved in spite of what failures and defects there are in us.

Jesus as the Rose of Sharon not only reminds us of God's love and availability; Jesus our Rose is also our delight. Roses are a delight to behold and to smell. We enjoy food that we eat for its taste and for its strengthening nutrition. We enjoy music for its rhythm or for the comfort of the memories it conjures, for the calm it brings, for the release it offers whatever our mood. But a rose—a rose is enjoyed for itself. It's all right to serve the Lord out of a sense of duty. It's all right to love the Lord because of what he does for us. But the greatest joy in life and faith comes when we just delight in the Lord for the fragrant beauty of who he is. What can Jesus, the Rose of Sharon, mean to you? He is not only our greatest lover, who is always available and accessible to us, he is also our greatest joy.

We pray to him not only because we need something; we just delight in being in his presence: For in his presence "there is fullness of joy" (Psalm 16:11). We read the Bible not only because we need to, but because we delight in God's Word: "Happy are those who do not follow the advice of the wicked,… but their delight is in the law of the LORD, and on his law they meditate day and night" (Psalm 1:1-2). Our delight, our greatest joy is praise: "Worship the LORD with gladness; come into his presence with singing.… Give thanks to him, bless his name" (Psalm 100:2,4).

As the Rose of Sharon, Jesus is my delight, my love, and perhaps above all, he is *mine*, available and accessible whether I am in need of his power, his comfort, or simply the joy of his presence: "O taste and see that the LORD is good" (Psalm 34:8)—*all* the time!

✕ 4 ✕

Lily of the Valley

Song of Solomon 2:1

I am a rose of Sharon,
a lily of the valleys.
(Song of Solomon 2:1)

THE LILY OF THE VALLEY IS ONE OF OUR MORE POPULAR biblical descriptions of Christ in the black church—so popular, in fact, that it has become part of our cultural idiom. I've often wondered why Jesus is referred to as the Lily of the Valley. There is an actual flower that grows in the mountains from Virginia to South Carolina called the lily of the valley. Although this North American version is a different species than that which is described in the Bible, both flowers are found in places where a more delicate flower would not survive: in shady places and on sandy and rocky ground. In the Bible, valleys represent life's difficult places. David said, "Even though I walk through the darkest valley"—the King James Version says "the valley of the shadow of death"—"I fear no evil; for you are with me" (Psalm 23:4). Thus, when we talk about Jesus Christ as Lily of the Valley, we are talking about someone who is with us in life's difficult, low, rocky, and barren places.

We who can be assured that we are not alone as we go through life's valleys are blessed indeed, because such is not always the case. When Job hit his rocky place, his good friends accused him of unrighteousness, and his closest companion told him to curse God and die. After betraying Christ and remorsefully trying to return the thirty pieces of silver, Judas received no sympathy or understanding from those who had encouraged him to be untrue to the best person he had ever known. Feeling lonely and desperately alone, he committed suicide. When the prodigal's money ran out, so did his friends. In a strange land and a time of famine, no one gave him anything to eat. Don't ever measure your popularity and your quotient of friends when you're on the mountain peaks of success ... when you are in a position of power and people need you. The true measure of your popularity and the test of people's friendship come when you're in one of life's difficult or rocky valleys.

When I was a college president, my phone rang off the hook, and everywhere I went my brethren greeted me warmly. But when I lost my job, I was surprised how my busy phone suddenly became silent and many of my brethren avoided me or acted as if they were afraid to speak to me. People who are sick or retired, or those who have made mistakes and shamed themselves often have the same experience. However, if we know Jesus as Lily of the Valley, we know that, although others leave, we have a very-present help who will never forsake us, one who will be with us through the valleys and rocky places.

Never underestimate the importance of the presence of Christ in life's low valleys. During my valley period, I almost had a nervous breakdown. One night I actually felt my mind leaving me and I was too scared to pray. I almost lost my mind, but I didn't. Somebody else can say: "I almost died, but I didn't." "I almost strayed, but I didn't." "I almost gave up, but I didn't." "I almost went back to the bottle or back to drugs, but I didn't." What counts in life is not what we *almost* did, but what we *actually* did. When we were at the edge, what kept us from going off the deep end? We had a presence that wouldn't let us go. Even when we can't hold on any longer, Jesus, the Lily of the Valley, keeps holding us through life's difficult places.

Lilies don't just exist in the valley; they *grow* in the valley. Whatever beauty they have, whatever fragrance they give, whatever blessings they bestow, they do so in the valley. Jesus as Lily of the Valley means we not only have a never-failing presence in life's difficult places, but we have power to keep growing and keep going in the valley. The issue is not just our making it through, but whether we will be stronger or weaker, better or bitter, more alive or more dead, on the other side. When there is the presence of the Lily, we can keep growing and emerge stronger on the other side of the midnight moment.

I have always thought that knowing Jesus was a sweet experience, but when my father died I discovered the real joy of knowing the Lord. My father died on a Tuesday in May. We held his home-going service on Saturday in the church where he had been pastor. The very next day I had to stand in the pulpit where he had stood so many times before, the very pulpit from which he had been eulogized less than twenty-four hours before, and I had to preach. My text was Nehemiah 6:3, which says, "I am doing a great work and I cannot come down." My subject was "I Can't Stop Now." Instead of becoming weaker in that moment of grief and loss, I stood in strength. Jesus, the Lily of the Valley, helped me to grow stronger. That's what Jesus will do for you. If you know him, he will help you to keep growing. Your troubles become your testimony. Your burdens become your blessings. Your obstacles become your opportunities. Your hardships become your helps. Your mountains become your miracles. Your valleys become your victories, and your crosses become your crowns.

Lilies transform barren valley floors and rocky slopes into places of peace and beauty. When you have the presence of Christ in your difficult places, you not only have power to go through and keep growing, you also can have peace in the valley. When you know you're not alone, you can have peace. When you know that the one who is with you gives you power to grow, you can have peace in your valley. When you know that the same one who clothes the lilies of the field with a dignity that not even Solomon's splendor can match, you can have peace in your valley. When you know that the Lord hasn't brought you this far to leave you, you can have peace in your valley.

Across the ages I hear Jesus, our Lily of the Valley, saying, "Peace I leave with you; my peace I give to you. I do not give to you as the world gives. Do not let your hearts be troubled, and do not let them be afraid" (John 14:27). That's what Thomas Dorsey was talking about when he sang:

> *There'll be peace in the valley for me someday*
> *There'll be peace in the valley for me I pray*
> *No more sorrow, no more sadness,*
>   *no more trouble there'll be*
> *There'll be peace in the valley for me.*

The Gate

John 10:1-3,7-8

So again Jesus said to them,
"Very truly, I tell you, I am the gate
for the sheep." (John 10:7)

MOST OF US ARE FAMILIAR WITH THE KING JAMES VERSION'S use of the word *door*. However, when we consider the context of Jesus' words, we realize he was referring to the entrance of a sheepfold. Sheepfolds had gates rather than doors. Thus, the translation of the New Revised Standard Version and other modern versions of the word as "gate" are more technically correct. Either way, though, gates and doors operate on the same principle.

When we use the image of Jesus as the Gate as found in John's Gospel, we are reminded that a gate has two simultaneous purposes: it opens and it shuts. A closed gate keeps some things or persons out, while also keeping other things and persons in.

Jesus as the Gate closes or shuts out some things. Often when people apply for a job or run for political office, a background check is done. If anything bad is found, the person has to explain the whats, the whys, and the wherefores. Many persons have found themselves shamed into silence or stumbling for words as they tried to explain some incident or period of time in their past. We are all aware that at the most unexpected and embarrassing times our past can suddenly rise up to haunt us. However, if Jesus is our personal Savior we don't have to run from our past or feel ashamed of it. Once we accept Jesus in our life, no one has a right to dig into our past and throw it up in our face to shame us. We have a right to look at our foes and those would who dredge up our past and say without flinching, "You are correct in what you have found and in what you are saying. My past is what it is, but Jesus has shut the gate on my past. He has saved and redeemed me from my past. The person, the habit, the behavior, the weakness you described are no more. That's over and done with. That's yesterday's news. Let me give you a current 'bio.' Let me tell you about who I am now." When Jesus is the Gate in your life, what once made you feel ashamed becomes your testimony about the reality of Jesus' saving power.

Now once Jesus shuts the gate, he keeps it shut. That does not mean that you don't tell your story about what the Lord has done for you. But you tell it without guilt. Don't keep beating yourself up over your past mistakes. Jesus the Gate has shut the door on them, and so when those mistakes raise their heads, what you ought to feel is not agonizing guilt, but amazing grace. There may be some trembling about the chances we have taken, but there ought to be more thanks-giving about the choices you have now. When Jesus is your Gate, you don't have to live with a sigh of regret; you can live with a song of redemption. When Jesus is your Gate, you don't have to be haunted by your past; you have holiness in the present. When Jesus is your Gate, you don't have to live in fear of the past; you can live with faith in the present.

A good friend once said to me, "My only regret is that I waited so long to come in through the Gate." I told him, "At least you had sense enough to come in. When Jesus knocked on the door of your heart, at least you had sense enough to answer. There are many who haven't answered yet. And since you've been in—you've been in. You've kept the Gate shut tight against your past, and you've been living in the joy of your new reality and serving the Lord with everything you have." Once Jesus shuts the door, keep the gate shut.

Keep the Gate shut on guilt. Keep the Gate shut on sin. You know what your weakness is; quit flirting with it. You know fire burns; quit playing with it. Keep the Gate shut on that crowd that means you no good. Once the Lord has delivered you from that abusive and bad relationship, take your key back and keep the Gate shut.

Now, as the Gate, Jesus not only shuts some things out; he also opens the door to some other things. As much as we rejoice in what Jesus has shut out of our lives, we are most grateful about what he has opened to us. Some people emphasize what Jesus has shut the door on—what they *don't* do. I like to talk about what Jesus the Gate has opened up to us—what we *can* do.

23

Jesus has opened up access to the throne of grace. When our sins make us unworthy to come to God, we can plead the blood of Jesus that cleanses us and thus find help at the throne of mercy in our time of need. He has opened up to us the power and joy of forgiveness. We have been able to pray for people we didn't think we'd ever pray for, and we can get rid of some feelings we've had that we didn't think we would ever be rid of. We know we couldn't have done it on our own. Only Jesus opening our hearts to forgiveness could have produced that change.

Jesus the Gate has opened the way to true joy. We thought the world offered a good time on a Friday or Saturday night. But no good time can match the good time we can have in church when the Spirit is right and Jesus has opened our heart.

Jesus the Gate has opened to us power to defy the devil. We don't have to live in fear of evil. In the name of Jesus we can back the devil down and put him where he belongs. Not behind us where he can stab us, not beside us where he can seduce us, or in front of us to lead us astray, but underneath our feet, conquered and confined.

Jesus the Gate has opened for us virtual wellsprings of self-confidence. Don't tell *us* what we can't do with Jesus in our life. We really do believe in the testimony of Paul: "I can do all things through him who strengthens me" (Philippians 4:13). What's more, Jesus has opened for us the gates of life eternal: "We know that if the earthly tent we live in is destroyed, we have a building from God, a house not made with hands, eternal in the heavens" (2 Corinthians 5:1).

Jesus is the Gate—not a gate but *the* Gate. Why? Because he's the *living* Gate. Buddha is dead. Mohammed is dead. Moses is dead. Jesus is a living presence. When we have living problems, we need a living presence. When we have living sin, we need a living savior. When there is a living devil, we need a living Door. When the fiery trials of this life are about to overtake us, we need more than a commandment or a principle or a book that goes only so far and stops. We need the living presence that bridges the gap between where we are and where we need to go. We need Jesus, the living Gate that can open what no man or woman can shut, and shut what no man or woman can open. We need Jesus.

✕✕ **6** ✕✕

The Resurrection and the Life

John 11:20-26

Jesus said to her,
"I am the resurrection and the life.
Those who believe in me, even though they die,
will live, and everyone who lives and
believes in me will never die.
Do you believe this?" (John 11:25-26)

THESE OFTEN QUOTED VERSES HAVE TO BE ABOUT MORE than physical death. If this text refers only to physical death, then it would have very little meaning to most of us. Very few if any of us know of Jesus as the Resurrection and the Life as Mary and Martha came to know him. Very few if any of us have had the experience of seeing someone die, remain dead four days, and then be brought back to life. And if any of us *did* see someone raised from the dead, we would do what no human being has been known to do: we would outrun the speed of light! Thus, although the immediate context for this verse is the physical death of Lazarus, we understand that the words have a much broader meaning.

To begin with, physical death is not the only death that we encounter. Some of us are spiritually dead: we function on routine and habit. Because we go through the motions of religion, we think that we are alive. The inner workings of a clock are constantly moving, but a clock is not alive. An automobile and airplane are built for the sole purpose of providing movement at great speeds, but an automobile and airplane are not alive. There is a difference between the mechanics of motion and the movement of life. Some of us go through the motions, but we have no life. Some of us go through the motions of religion, but we have no life. We may go through the motions of a marriage or of a significant relationship, but we have no life. Some of us go through the motions of sex, but there is no life in the intimacy.

Never get the motions of sex confused with making love. All you need for sex are the appropriate body parts, but you need life for love. You need heart and soul for love. That's why some of us are always putting ourselves in a position to be used and abused. We believe that the way you get love is through your limbs, but limbs can work mechanically. Limbs without life, heart, soul, and commitment are just going through the motions. If there is nothing beyond the physical, then when you close your limbs or put your limb away, you will still be love-starved and spirit-dead. The next time somebody tells you, "If you love me, you will do [blank] for me," you tell them that there is a difference between limbs and love and that you are into love and not just into motion. I know people whose limbs are not very functional, but they have love and that love makes them almost glow.

Every day some of us go through the motions in our job or in our school, but we have no life. Then there are those who are dead to conscience. The first time we did something wrong, conscience screamed so loudly that we thought we would shrivel from shame. But after repeating our transgression over and over again, we don't even hear conscience speak anymore. We may talk about wrong and right, but conscience is dead in us and our motions of righteousness have no life.

To those of us who have a mechanical existence of motion and no life, to those who have become dead to conscience, Jesus has a word: "I am the resurrection and the life...." Note that there is a difference between life through resurrection and life through giving birth. To give birth is to bring new life into the world. To resurrect is to bring back to life what has died. Those of us who have never known Jesus as our personal Lord and Savior and who have never received the baptism of the Holy Spirit—those persons need to be born anew in Christ. But many of us who have already been born again need resurrection. We need to find again what we once had. We need the restoration of what has been lost. We need another chance at what the death of going through the motions has taken away.

When Jesus spoke to Nicodemus and told him that he must be born again—that was life through birth. But when Jesus released the man of his demonic legion—that was life through resurrection. When Jesus called Matthew, Thomas, and others to be disciples—that was birth. But on the day of Pentecost when the Holy Spirit came upon those disciples—that was resurrection. When Jesus preached the Sermon on the Mount to the masses—that was birth. But when he told the woman caught in adultery, "Go in peace and sin no more"—that was resurrection. When Jesus healed the man born blind—that was birth. But when he gave living water to a much-married Samaritan woman at Jacob's well—that was resurrection. When Jesus called Simon Peter to preach—that was birth. But when he forgave Simon Peter his three denials of the Lord— that was resurrection. When Jesus called Saul on the Damascus Road—that was birth. But when he called Lazarus back from the grave—that was resurrection.

Some of us need resurrection. Like Lazarus, we need to be called back from the grave—back from darkness to light, back from bondage to freedom, back from where the majority consensus has placed us, back from an impossible situation and undeliverable circumstance. We need to be called back, from death into life.

When our favorite phrase is "we used to," we need resurrection. When our favorite song is "What peaceful hours I once enjoyed, so sweet their memories still," we need resurrection. When all we do is go through the motions, we need resurrection. When our love has waxed cold and we're afraid to trust anybody, we need resurrection. When we've been hurt and can't get over it, abused and can't recover from it, swamped by sin and can't repent of it—we need resurrection.

The good news is, I know who is Resurrection. There are a lot of things I don't know, but I do know—not *what* is but *who* is Resurrection. You see, our faith is not just about believing some things; it's about knowing somebody—and I know who is Resurrection. I may not be able to quote verse and chapter of the Bible like some people, but I know who is Resurrection. I may not have all the gifts that some others may have, but I know who is Resurrection. I may not be as smart or as righteous as some others, but I know who is Resurrection. When I've sinned and fallen short of God's glory, when I've gone as far as I can go and don't have strength to go any further, I know who is Resurrection.

Jesus said, "I am the resurrection and the life. Those who believe in me, even though they die, they will live." *If* you believe… "Believe my blood can cleanse you. Believe my Word is true. Believe my presence is always with you. Believe my power can restore you. Believe my intercession will bring mercy. Believe that one day I'm coming back for you—and you will have resurrection power."

Resurrection power means bouncing-back power. Some people will use an expression when you ask them how they feel. They'll say, "I'm alive and kicking." That's your testimony when Jesus, the Resurrection and the Life, resurrects you—"I'm alive and kicking." People have been digging ditches and setting traps, but that's all right. With Jesus in my life, "I'm alive and kicking." I've had to come up the rough side of the mountain. Sometimes I didn't know how I was going to make it over, but through it all, "I'm alive and kicking." They thought they had buried me and that I was over and done with, but I know who the Resurrection and Life is, so "I'm alive and kicking."

⚮ 7 ⚮

Living Water

John 4:7-15

*Jesus answered her, "If you knew the gift of God,
and who it is that is saying to you, 'Give me a
drink,' you would have asked him, and
he would have given you living water."*
(John 4:10)

WATER, WHICH HAS A CHEMICAL FORMULA OF H_2O, IS critical for life. Our bodies are composed mostly of water. That's why dehydration—the body's lack of water—is such a critical condition for us; without sufficient water in our body, we die. Thus, when Jesus describes himself as Living Water, he is saying that our very survival depends upon his presence in our lives.

To understand this point we have to remember how we are made. We are more than merely physiological creatures: we are human beings with souls and minds as well as bodies. We are so much more than physical bodies that when we live

31

only to satisfy the physical appetite, we cheapen all that we are—and more than we can comprehend with our finite minds. As human beings, we have a little bit of heaven in us as well as earth. That's another reason why Jesus is so critical to our existence; even more than we have, Jesus has a dual nature—divine and human—incarnating both heaven and earth. As such, he is uniquely qualified to live with us as a human and then to lift us with him as God; to cry with us as a human and then to carry us as God; to suffer with us as a human and then to save us as God; to tackle problems with us as a human and then to transcend those problems for us as God; to help us as a human and then to heal us as God; to die with us as a human and then to deliver us as God.

In his humanity and in his divinity, Jesus, like water, is indispensable to us. However, let us note the kind of water he is: Living Water, not stagnant water. Stagnant water just sits and becomes stale and unfit for use, contaminated with bacteria and polluted with debris. When Jesus, our Living Water, floods our life, we are compelled to do more than sit around and wait for a trumpet to call us to heaven. If we did that, we would become stale—and one thing that's killing a lot of churches today is too much staleness: stale preaching, stale praying, stale singing, stale testi-lying, stale form and ritual, stale people doing nothing but sitting around from week to week battling over turf, titles, offices, seats, uniforms, and anniversary dates. Do you know any stale Christians who have been doing nothing for so long that they have become unfit for service or vision? Jesus, the Living Water, carries us along, compelling us to do so much more than sit and stagnate!

Jesus is Living Water, not frozen water. Some Christians are as cold as ice. And I'm not talking about their cold worship style but their cold-heartedness. Some people will "Jesus, Jesus, Jesus" you to death, but they have no compassion. They are self-centered and self-righteous, not willing to go out of their way to help anybody unless they can see how they will get the benefit. They are cold toward the homeless, cold toward unwed mothers, cold toward these who have been addicted, cold toward gay people, cold toward those who have been in trouble, cold toward anybody who does not measure up to their standards. Jesus offered Living Water to a woman scorned as promiscuous. We don't have to agree with people's choices in order to have some compassion and caring, because, as quiet as it's kept, the truth is that "but for the grace of God," there go we all.

Jesus is Living Water, not boiling water. Some people's testimony has so much fire and so much heat that it scorches the ones who need the Living Water most of all. Quit sending everybody to hell. Every word out of our mouths does not have to be "Hallelujah" and "Praise the Lord," and we don't have to stay in church all the time. Even Jesus didn't do that! Zacchaeus never would have been saved and the woman with the issue of blood never would have been healed if Jesus had been in church all the time. It's all right to have fun. If you're on your way to heaven, you ought to enjoy the trip. Don't become so hot and holy that you lose your sense of humor. Don't become so hot that you scald people with your touch, attitude, and conversation and turn them off instead of on. Jesus, the Living Water, is not about fanaticism but balance.

Jesus is Living Water, not evaporated water. Steam is a form of water, but the problem is that it evaporates; you can't get a hold of it. Some people have plenty of praise but when there is work to be done, their religion seems to evaporate; you can't get a hold of them. They can show up on Sunday morning to sing or for their anniversary or to wear the new uniform, but not for the rehearsal or the meeting after the big day is over. They just seem to evaporate; you can't get a hold of them. Some people can out sing, out shout, out pray, out dance, out speak-in-tongues everybody else, but when offering time comes, when it's time to tithe, their religion seems to evaporate. When the sick need to be visited, when a child needs to be cared for, when the hungry need to be fed, they evaporate. As long as things are going well in life or going their way in the church, they have great commitment. However, let a little trouble arise, let a disagreement occur, let them lose their office or take offense, and like steam they evaporate.

Jesus as Living Water is *not* ice or steam or boiling hot. Nor is our Living Water stagnant. Jesus as Living Water is fresh, he's flowing, and he's free! For water to be fresh, it has to flow, and in order to flow it has to be free. I don't know about you, but I have given Jesus permission to flow freely through my life. Whatever he wants me to be, I'll be. Wherever he wants me to go, I'll go. Whatever he wants me to do, I'll do. Whatever he wants me to say, I'll say. I want him to be free in my life—free to flow and refresh. That's what so much of our religion and so many of our lives need—a freshening up. We go through the same old motions with the same people who talk about the same things and fight over the same issues year in and year out. Some of us haven't had a fresh idea or thought in years. No wonder we're stagnant or frozen or boiling over or evaporating. It's time for us to freshen up.

Jesus is about freshness. When he talked about being born again, that was freshness. When he talked about new wine in new wineskins, that was freshness. When he called Lazarus from the tomb and gave blind Bartimaeus his sight, the Samaritan woman her dignity, and the man at the pool of Bethesda the activity of his limbs—that was freshness. When he talked about the cross being an emblem of salvation instead of an instrument of shame—that was freshness. Paul declared his knowledge that Jesus is in the freshening-up business when he said, "If anyone is in Christ, there is a new creation; everything old has passed away; see, everything has become new!" (2 Corinthians 5:17).

The freshness of Jesus as Living Water comes from the freedom to flow—to flow in the Spirit through the lives of those who ask for that refreshing drink. His peace doesn't trickle; it flows. His promises don't drip; they flow. His forgiveness doesn't seep; it flows. His love does not freeze; it flows. His presence does not evaporate; it flows. His cleansing does not stagnate; it flows. No wonder somebody said:

Praise God from whom all blessings flow,
Praise him, all creatures here below,
Praise him above, ye heavenly host,
Praise Father, Son, and Holy Ghost.

✕ **8** ✕

Bread of Life and the Living Bread

John 6:48-51

"I am the bread of life.... I am the living bread that came down from heaven. Whoever eats of this bread will live forever; and the bread that I will give for the life of the world is my flesh."
(John 6:48,51)

THE STORY IS TOLD OF A CHICKEN AND A PIG THAT WERE walking down the road discussing the farmer's breakfast. The chicken suggested that they serve bacon and eggs, but the pig objected. So the chicken suggested that they serve the farmer sausage and eggs, but the pig objected again. Then the chicken suggested that they serve ham and eggs, but the pig objected again, even more vehemently. Finally, the chicken asked the pig why he was being so disagreeable. The pig told the chicken, "Your suggestions require that you make only a contribution, but they require total commitment from me."

When Jesus called himself the Bread of Life, he was talking about making more than a contribution to our salvation—to our deliverance, our empowerment, our life. Lest we forget, nobody eats a whole loaf of bread. We bruise the bread before we eat it. We cut it, tear it, or break it so that we can get the portion that we can handle. Breaking or bruising something that is alive involves pain and suffering. Thus, Jesus was talking about more than a casual contribution when he told the disciples, "This is my body, which is broken for you" (1 Corinthians 11:24, KJV). The prophet was talking about more than a mere contribution when he said of our Redeemer, "He was wounded for our transgressions, he was bruised for our iniquities…" (Isaiah 53:5, KJV).

When Jesus called himself the Bread of Life, he was making more than a contribution. For us to be nourished and strengthened by bread it must be in us; it must be consumed. We do not eat living wheat. For us to have bread, the wheat has to give up its life at the harvest so that it can be threshed, ground, and baked. Anything that goes into us dies in the process of nourishing us.

What does Jesus as the Bread of Life mean to us? It means we have somebody in our life and on our side who is totally and completely, without reservation or equivocation, committed to us. It means we have someone so committed to us that he will not only allow himself to be beaten and broken for us and to suffer for us, but that he will also die for us. I don't know about you, but I never cease to marvel at how much Jesus loves each of us, how much he is committed to each of us, and how much that love cost him—his own life.

If I would go around the church and ask the question "What is Jesus' greatest gift to you?" I would get a number of answers: salvation, healing, a second chance, peace, wisdom, love, forgiveness, power, etc. And as good and true as those answers are, they would all be wrong. Jesus' greatest gift to us is he himself. If Jesus had not given himself to us totally and completely, he would not have been able to give us those other precious gifts of healing, salvation, peace, and so on. Everything we receive from Jesus is secondary to his total and primary gift: himself.

A father who was caring for his daughter discovered that they were out of bread. He told the little girl that he was going to the corner store to pick up the bread for their sandwiches and that he would be right back. He was gone only about five minutes when he heard an explosion. As he ran out of the store and looked up the street, he saw the apartment building in which he and his family lived engulfed in flames. He also saw his little daughter standing on the ledge of the third-story window. The father ran to the building and yelled up to his daughter, "Jump, baby, jump! Daddy will catch you." The little girl jumped and landed in her father's arms, but the weight of the jump caused him to stumble backward. He fell to the curb and broke his neck. He looked up into the eyes of his daughter and said with his last breath, "When your mother gets home, tell her I died in order that you might live." That was the kind of total commitment and sacrificial love that the Lord Jesus had for us on Calvary.

Why would Jesus make such a total commitment? For two reasons. First, because he loves us. As stubborn, selfish, egotistical, and disobedient as we are—he loves us. "Jesus loves me, this is I know," not only because the Bible tells us so, but because Calvary tells us so. A crown of thorns tells us so. Nail prints in his hands and feet tell us so. A spear in his side tells us so. Stripes on his back tell us so.

When I think about the total commitment it cost Jesus to be the Bread of Life, I understand in a new way what Paul was talking about when he said, "Love … bears all things, believes all things, hopes all things, endures all things. Love never ends." Jesus as the Bread of Life signifies that kind of enduring love, that he was willing to be broken for us.

But Jesus is totally committed to us not only because he loves us, but also because he knows our possibilities—knows them better than we do ourselves. When we've tried and failed, when our best doesn't seem good enough, Jesus is that presence in our lives who tells us, "You can do it." When we injure ourselves, he picks us up and carries us. That's why he is not only the Bread of Life that was broken for us on Calvary; he is also the Living Bread, the resurrected bread that is able still to bless and keep. When we come to the end of our journey, it will be the Living Bread who will stand beside us when we get our medal. What, then, is our response to the Bread of Life and the Living Bread?

First, we must recognize that if Jesus is so totally committed to us, then we must be worthwhile. When we begin to think of ourselves as nobodies, as failures, we must remember that if Jesus believes in us as much as he does, then we must be worthwhile. No matter how much we mess up or fall down, if Jesus believes in us and is committed to us as much as he is, we must be worthwhile.

Second, we must realize that such a total commitment of love and life demands an equally total commitment in response. When we think about Jesus' total commitment to us, can we do any less than love him and serve him totally? When I was younger I used to hear older people say, "Who wouldn't want to serve a God like that?" "For God so loved the world"—who wouldn't want to serve a God like that? "In this is love, not that we loved God but that he loved us and sent his Son"—who wouldn't want to serve a God like that? "And when I think that God, his Son not sparing, sent him to die, I scarce can take it in"—who wouldn't want to serve a God like that? "In my Father's house there are many dwelling places. If it were not so, would I have told you that I go to prepare a place for you?"—who wouldn't want to serve a God like that?

When Isaac Watts surveyed the wondrous cross, he responded with these words: "Were the whole realm of nature mine, That were a present far too small: Love so amazing, so divine, Demands my soul, my life, my all."

May our response be as total and our commitment be as complete, that accepting the Bread of Life broken for us, we will partake of the Living Bread and never die.

✂ **9** ✂

The True Vine

John 15:1-5

*"I am the vine, you are the branches.
Those who abide in me and I in them
bear much fruit, because apart from me
you can do nothing."* (John 15:5)

WHEN AFRICANS WERE BROUGHT TO THESE SHORES TO BE enslaved, a sustained and systematic effort was made to cut us off from all of the links with our African past so that we would feel alone and friendless in a hostile world. Thus, we would be completely dependent upon our slave masters for everything—survival, sustenance, and self-definition. The existential reality of being uprooted and disconnected was at the heart of the spiritual our ancestors sang: "Sometimes I feel like a motherless child a long ways from home."

When we are trying to serve the Lord, do the right thing, make something of ourselves and of our lives, one of the most effective ways the devil has of discouraging us is to make us feel forsaken, lonely, and misunderstood. When I was in Georgia, we used to have a saying: "It's just me one." If Satan can ever get us to feel that "it's just me one," that we are dangling out here by ourselves with nobody but ourselves to really depend upon or to understand us, then he has gone a long way toward crippling and capturing us.

It is in these moments, when we are tempted to believe that we are out there on our own, that Jesus' statement "I am the true vine, you are the branches" has special meaning. Being a branch in relation to a vine means that we have connections. We are not out there by ourselves. We are not alone in life. We don't have to depend only upon our own strength and our own knowledge to make it. We are connected to somebody: we belong to the True Vine.

In life we are told that certain people are "well connected." That is to say that they have the kind of political, social, or financial contacts that can get things done. When you are a follower of Jesus, don't underestimate your connections. To be a follower of Jesus means that you are connected to somebody who *was* before there was a when or a where, a then or a there; a somebody who *was* before "the morning stars sang together and all the heavenly beings shouted for joy" (Job 38:7). You are connected to somebody who is not only the Alpha and the Omega, but the Nu as well. *Alpha* and *omega* are the first and last letters of the Greek alphabet; *nu* is the middle letter. Thus, Jesus is not only somebody who will be with us in the beginning when we're born and at the end when death comes. He abides with us in all that is between ... in the middle. In the middle, when temptation comes to turn us around. In the middle, when Satan attacks to dismantle and destroy. In the middle, when friends become few. In the middle, when resources run short. In the middle, when the unexpected shakes the foundations of our lives. In the middle, when relationships are severed. Yes, in the middle. Therefore, we can continue to abide in Jesus. He is sufficient for whatever comes between our beginning and our ending.

Jesus is not only *a* vine to which we are connected, but he is the True Vine. In life we will establish a number of connections—business, family, church, social, and so on. However, Jesus as the True Vine abides when other connections fail. When I was out of a job, I had good connections, but none of my connections were able to deliver me. They tried but they just couldn't. However, because I was connected to Jesus, he opened doors that no one could shut.

As a follower of Jesus, as a branch grafted to the True Vine, never underestimate your connections. When you know Jesus, you know somebody who is able to still storms, defeat demons, silence adversaries, make something out of nothing, and make much out of little.

Jesus as the True Vine is reason for confidence, yes, but also for caution. When Jesus is the True Vine and we are branches, we are not only connected; we are cut. Jesus said, "I am the true vine, and my Father is the vinegrower. He removes every branch in me that bears no fruit. Every branch that bears the fruit he prunes to make it bear more fruit" (John 15:1-2). Being a branch connected to the True Vine of Jesus means that at some time or another we will be cut. The world will cut us sometimes; family and friends will cut us; church people will cut us; the devil will cut us. Even Jesus was cut: "He was wounded for our transgressions" (Isaiah 53:5, KJV). When the risen Jesus appeared before his disciples, he showed them his cuts: nail-scarred hands and a pierced side. Paul said, "Henceforth, let no man trouble me: for I bear in my body the marks of the Lord Jesus" (Galatians 6:17, KJV). You can't be a Christian without some cut-marks. Cross bearing will leave its mark on you.

However, what is most disturbing about this passage is not the news that we will be cut, but that the heavenly Vinegrower is doing the cutting. I expect the world and the devil and jealous humans to cut, but not God. Why would God cut us or allow us to be cut? Well, we have to understand that God is not a lumberjack but a tree surgeon—or to take it a step further, God is not a mugger but a surgeon. A mugger will cut with a knife to destroy, but a surgeon will take the same knife to heal. When a surgeon uses a knife, he or she is operating to remove something malignant or to restore what was injured. When the cut is made, it is painful, but in the long run, the surgery is best for us.

"Every branch that bears fruit he prunes to make it bear more fruit." That's why we are cut: to bear more fruit. In other words, we are cut to conquer. To be a branch connected to the True Vine of Jesus means that we are connected and we are cut, but that's not all—we are also conquerors. No tree can bear fruit without some cutting. No plant can grow without some watering, even if the water is our tears. No seed can grow unless it is buried—but when you are buried, know that it's not forever. You are buried to rise again! We are cut to conquer.

Cut down a lone cedar and it will die, but cut back a branch that is connected to a vine and it will come back stronger. As a follower of Jesus you are connected to the True Vine. So when you are cut down with problems, you will conquer and come back stronger with prayer. When you are cut down with trouble, you will come back stronger with a testimony. When you are cut down with criticism, you will come back stronger with Christ. When you are cut down with heartache, you will come back stronger with hope. When you are cut down with viciousness, you will come back stronger with a victory, a victory claimed in the name of Jesus, who is the True Vine.

✕✕ 10 ✕✕

The Way

John 14:6

Jesus said to him, "I am the way, and the truth, and the life. No one comes to the Father except through me." (John 14:6)

IN JOHN 14:6, JESUS DECLARES THREE NAMES FOR HIM-self. The first is the word *way,* which is a noun, and one of its meanings is "a path or course leading from one place to another." Jesus as the Way tells us that he is a means of egress or access. Every living creature is going somewhere. There are times when we may feel that our lives are standing still, but no life is ever really stationary. From youth to old age, from health to sickness to health again, from ignorance to education, from innocence to experience, from the cradle to the grave, all of us are on our way somewhere—whether we are willing travelers or not!

Although we may have little input about the fact that we are going *somewhere,* we do have input about the quality of our life's journey. We even can have input about the length of our journey. Some of us are hastening our journey's end. With the decisions we make about what we eat, drink, smoke, ingest, and about what we do and how we live, we can have some input not only about the character or quality of our journey, but also about the length of our journey. We can look at some people and know that unless they change their ways, they won't be around very long.

So since we are on a course—a path or journey—from one place to the other, Jesus says, "I am the way. I am your means of egress and access." Jesus is the way out. Some of us are trying to get out of something. We're sure life has something better to offer us, if we could just get out of where we are. We feel like we're in quicksand: the more we struggle the deeper we sink. But before we can get ahead, we have to do some getting out—out of depression, out of sin, out of some hellish relationships, out of some ways of thinking, out of some guilt, out of some bitter memories.

If we're trying to get out of something, Jesus says, "I am the way out." Well, before the prodigal son could get out of the hog pen, he had to be prepared to wave goodbye to the hogs (see Luke 15:11-19). Jesus can be the way out if we're prepared to do some waving. Are we really prepared to wave goodbye to the hogs we've grown accustomed to lying down with, living with, and hanging around with? Some of us have become comfortable with the pigs, so comfortable that, with as much complaining as we do, whenever we have the opportunity to leave them, we choose to stay with them. Others of us have a love/hate relationship with the hogs.

Some things about the hogs we hate, but other things we love. So rather than leave what gives us some joy and security, we choose to lie down and wallow with what we hate.

The prodigal son didn't wave goodbye just to *some* of the hogs in the pen, but to *all* of the hogs in the pen. The problem for some of us is that we want Jesus to be the way out, but we want to keep one or two of our favorite hogs with us. Some of us may ask, "What will I do without my hogs? How will I make it without my hogs?" Jesus says, "Trust me, follow me, lean on me. I am the way out."

Jesus is not only the way *out;* he is the way *to.* For the prodigal son to get back home, he had to follow a certain path. All roads from the hog pen didn't lead to where he was trying to go. That's why Jesus didn't say "I am *a* way" but said "I am *the* way." Jesus offers a specific route, gives specific instructions, makes specific promises, and guarantees speci-fic results. To get the results, you have to follow Jesus' way—the Way that *is* Jesus.

Most of us want Jesus to be our way *out,* but not our way *to.* We want him to get us out, but once we get out, we want to do our own thing and get to where we want to go by our own rules and our own ways. We have no problem with Jesus being Savior as a way *out,* but we do have problems with him being Lord of the way *to.*

But, if you can trust him to be your way out, then you can trust him to be the way to where you're trying to go. I once had a conversation with a young man who was a former drug addict and who was thinking about becoming a Muslim now that he was clean. I asked him, "Didn't Jesus get you off of drugs? Didn't he help you get your son back and find a new job and fresh start?" When he answered yes, I told him, "Well, if it ain't broke, don't fix it."

If the grace of the Lord Jesus was good enough to get you out of that mess, to get you off that sick bed, to keep you when you didn't have a job, to come to your aid when you yelled for help, then Jesus, the Way, is still able to give you new victories and take you where you need to go. No matter how long or winding the road, no matter if there are potholes and bumps in the road, even when roadblocks and detours obstruct the road—if he was able to get you out, then he's able to get you to.

But watch this: Jesus is not only the way out and the way to; he's the way *up*. When the father grabbed his prodigal son, he took him up in his arms and said, "Quickly, bring out a robe—the best one—and put it on him; put a ring on his finger and sandals on his feet.... for this son of mine was dead and is alive again; he was lost and is found!" (Luke 15:22,24). A good attorney will bail you out; a good friend will help you out; a good coach will work you out; a good parent will chew you out. So you can rely on other people and other things to get you out or to, but there comes a point when you get as far as they can take you—and you are not that much better off and you may be worse. In some cases, you might as well have stayed where you were! The movement has not been improvement or advancement, only change. I'm not for moving from one hog pen to another— one relationship to another, one church to another, one doctor to another, one job to another—with no advancement.

I'm interested in going up—not just down or around, frontward or backward, in or out—but up.

Jesus is the way up—up in our values, up in our vision, up in our faith; up in our living, up in our loving, up in our praying, up in our achieving; up in power and up in praise; up in new dimensions of the Spirit, up to the very throne of God.

Jesus said, "In my Father's house there are many dwelling places. If it were not so, would I have told you that I go to prepare a place for you? And if I go and prepare a place for you, I will come again and will take you to myself, so that where I am, there you may be also" (John 14:2-3). "I will come again…" he said. His promise is that if we have made him our way out, our way to, and our way up, then when he comes again, we will be caught up to meet him in the air and he will lead us to his Father's house, where he has prepared a place for us—and where he is the Way to get there.

11

The Truth

John 14:6

Jesus said to him, "I am the way, and the truth, and the life. No one comes to the Father except through me." (John 14:6)

THE SECOND OF JESUS' SELF-DECLARED NAMES IN JOHN 14:6 is the Truth—a profound name that can be unpacked as an acronym, examining each letter in the word and what it might represent. When Jesus calls himself the Truth, he is telling us fundamentally that he is trustworthy, or worthy of trust. That's what the first T in *truth* stands for. So many times we trust people who are not worthy of our trust. That's why some of us are so embittered, cynical, angry, suspicious, depressed, and fearful. We once trusted someone who proved to be unworthy of our trust, and we have vowed never to trust anybody else again. However, I bring you good news: Jesus, the Truth, is somebody worthy of your trust.

So, the next time you say "All men are dogs," remember that Jesus is a man. And if you say, "I'm talking about black men," I would remind you that Jesus is a black man. When

Daniel prophesied about the coming messiah in Daniel 7:9, he said, "...and the hair of his head [was] like pure wool." When John beholds the risen and exalted Christ in Revelation 1:14, he says that his hair was like white wool. The texture of black hair is essentially wooly. Jesus is a man—a black man—you can trust.

And to those who say "Women will do you in," I would remind you that Jesus was born of a woman—without the help of a man. Mary was a virgin when she conceived and bore Jesus. No matter what your experience has been, Jesus is the man, born of a woman, who is trustworthy.

How do we know Jesus is trustworthy? Jesus, the Truth, is trustworthy because he is right. That's what the R in *truth* means: right. Truth is that which is right. It is reality. What Jesus says is right and what he does is right. We follow his teachings not because they sound good or because they make sense, but because they are *right*. Jesus was right when he said, "Strive first for the kingdom of God and his righteousness" (Matthew 6:33). He was right when he said, a person's "life does not consist in the abundance of posessions" (Luke 12:15). He was right when he said, "Blessed are you when people revile you and persecute you and utter all kinds of evil against you falsely on my account" (Matthew 5:11). He was right when he said, "Love your enemies and pray for those who persecute you" (Matthew 5:44). Those black Christians are right who refuse to hate the racists that burned down their churches. Hate destroys the soul of those who hate, but love and prayer give us victory in our spirit. And once we get the victory in our spirit, we can shake off the evil that people do, shake it off like dust from our feet.

Jesus is right because of what he says and because of what he does. His contemporaries thought he was wrong to fellowship with tax collectors and sinners, wrong to heal on the Sabbath, wrong to speak with women and Gentiles, wrong to go to Jerusalem, wrong to accept death at the hands of religious and political leaders. They just didn't understand it then, but time has proved Jesus, the Truth, right. He was right when he went through so much, because if he hadn't, we wouldn't be able to sing a song that the angels cannot sing, "Redeemed, redeemed, I've been redeemed."

Jesus as the Truth is trustworthy. He is trustworthy because he is right. And the truth is trustworthy because it is unyielding. That's what the U in *truth* stands for—unyielding. A woman who enrolled in the same algebra course four times said she repeated the course so many times because she was tired of arguing with her classmates about everything in the world and wanted to study something she couldn't argue about. Mathematical computations do not yield to political pressure, money, or ravages of time. Two times two equals four, yesterday, today, tomorrow, and forever.

Jesus is Truth because, like mathematics, he is unyielding. Satan couldn't break him. Pilate couldn't impress him. Herod couldn't threaten him. Ananias and Caiaphas couldn't intimidate him. A bloodthirsty mob couldn't daunt him. A shout from a Palm Sunday crowd couldn't seduce him. Betrayal and denial by his own disciples couldn't dissuade him. He even refused to yield to death and the grave, because when they thought they had him, he rose to stoop no more! He is still Lord and Savior. No matter what the sin or the problem, no matter who is in the White House or the jail house, no matter how long you've been lost or how far down you have fallen, Jesus is still who he always has been—trustworthy, right, and unyielding. No matter whether you have a Ph.D. or no degree, whether you are a millionaire or a homeless beggar, you can count on the Truth: he is still Jesus, your Lord and Savior. After two thousand years, his blood can still cleanse and his words are still true.

Jesus is Truth because he is trustworthy, and he is trustworthy because he is right and unyielding. What's more, his truth is borne out in the testimonies of others. That's what the second T in *truth* stands for—testimonies. When we think about the millions of people who have believed in Jesus' name without regret, those who claim that nobody but Jesus healed them, saved them, delivered them, answered prayers for them, and made ways for them, all of them couldn't be wrong. Harriet Tubman, Sojourner Truth, Mahalia Jackson, and Fannie Lou Homer—as smart and shrewd as they were, they couldn't have been wrong about Jesus. George Washington Carver, Frederick Douglass, Martin Luther King—they couldn't have been wrong about Jesus. My great-grandmother with her shouts, my grandmother with her devotion, my daddy with his fire—all of whom have gone to glory—they couldn't have been wrong about Jesus. When I think about all those who have lived and died believing in him, and when I think about all those who are alive now who call him Savior and Lord—Jesus the Truth must be trustworthy.

Jesus is truth because he is trustworthy and he is trustworthy because he is right. He is unyielding throughout the testimonials about him—and he is truth because he is honorable. That's what the H in *truth* stands for—honorable. Jesus is honorable. If he says it, then he will do it, because he's honorable. He will never leave you nor forsake you, because he's honorable. He will not take advantage of your faith, love, and trust, because he's honorable. He will not put you out on a limb and then leave you hanging there to make it on your own. If he tells you to go, he'll go with you, because he's honorable. Even if you break your promises to him, Jesus the Truth will still be faithful to you, because he's honorable.

Jesus is Truth because truth is honorable, borne out in testimonies of unyielding righteousness and trustworthiness. And because Jesus the Truth is unyieldingly righteous and worthy of honor and trust, the holy angels join the testimony of saints here and gone, bowing with heaven and earth to adore him. And, it is at the name of Jesus, who is Truth, that one day every knee shall bow and every tongue confess to the glory of God that he is Lord.

12

The Life

John 14:6

Jesus said to him, "I am the way, and the truth, and the life. No one comes to the Father except through me." (John 14:6)

THE LAST OF JESUS' DESCRIPTIONS OF HIMSELF FOUND IN John 14:6 is "I am … the Life." Note the wording: *the* Life. Jesus does not describe himself simply as life. Any two creatures that copulate can produce life. We are aware that too many people—young people and people old enough to know better—produce life without really understanding the implications of what they are doing. So Jesus does not say, "I am life." Nor does he describe himself as "a life." The devil can offer *a* life. The prodigal son had a life in the hog pen. A prostitute or an abused woman has a life. A drug addict, drunkard, or derelict has a life. A slave has a life. Sick, white racists who burn down black churches have a life. Anyone who is breathing has life and a life.

Jesus identifies himself as more than life or a life; he declares, "I am *the* life." In other words, to talk about Jesus as the Life and the life that Jesus gives is to talk about quality and excellence. No blood can cleanse like his. No hand can heal or comfort or lift like his. No arm can enfold and no grasp can hold like his. No word has authority like his, at which storms become still and fig trees wither. No power works like his, which can multiply little into much and can cause devils to flee. No power can make the first the last and the last the first like his. Nobody can free like he can, because whomever the Son sets free is free indeed. Who wipes tears away like he can? Who can give peace in the midst of turmoil and bring blessings from burdens like he can? Who can redeem like he can? Who can make new like he can? Who can turn streetwalkers into evangelists and missionaries and make gutter dwellers into gospel preachers like he can? Who can bring resurrection from death like he can? And who can intercede for us at the throne of mercy like he can—and does?

What name is like *Jesus?* It is more inspiring than Caesar or Malcolm X; more musical than Beethoven or Mahalia Jackson; more victorious than Napoleon or Toussant L'Overture. The name of Jesus is more poetic than Milton or Paul Dunbar; more eloquent than Demosthenes or Barbara Jordan; more informed than Albert Einstein or Benjamin Banneker. The name of Jesus is more exalted than Joan of Arc or Martin Luther King Jr.; more excellent than Mother Teresa or Mary McLeod Bethune. No wonder when we think about his name all we can say is, "O Lord, how excellent is your name in all the earth."

Jesus as the Life brings into our lives the quality that makes the difference. Jesus as the Life so changes our lives that everybody around us can see something different about us. They may not like us but they can see an excellence, a different quality about us.

In a large stone cathedral in Europe, there was a large, magnificent pipe organ. It is said that on a Saturday afternoon, the sexton was was startled to hear footsteps echoing up the stone stairway. He had thought the doors were all locked and no one was around. He turned to see a man in slightly tattered traveling clothes coming toward him. "Excuse me, sir," the stranger said. "I have come from quite a distance to see the great organ in this cathedral. Would you mind opening the console so I might get a closer look at it?" The custodian at first refused, but the stranger seemed so eager and insistent that he finally gave in. "May I sit on the bench?" the stranger asked. The cathedral custodian met that request with absolute refusal, but again, the stranger was so persistent that the sexton gave in. "But only for a moment," he added.

The custodian noticed that the stranger seemed to be very much at home on the organ bench, so he was not completely surprised when the stranger next asked to be allowed to play the organ. "No! Definitely not!" said the custodian. "No one is allowed to play it except the cathedral organist." The man's face fell, and he assured the custodian that no damage would be done. Finally, the sexton relented. Overjoyed, the stranger began to play.

Suddenly, the cathedral was filled with the most beautiful music the custodian had ever heard. The music seemed to transport him heavenward. When the dowdy stranger stopped playing and started to leave, the custodian called out after him, "Wait. That was the most beautiful music I have ever heard in this cathedral. Who are you?" The stranger turned for just a moment as he replied, "Mendelssohn." The man was none other than Felix Mendelssohn, one of the greatest organists and composers of the nineteenth century. As the stunned janitor sat alone in the great cathedral with the sound of the beautiful organ music still ringing in his ears, he said softly to himself, "Just think: I almost kept the master from playing music in this cathedral."

Every one of us has the opportunity to have the Master of the universe, Jesus Christ, play his music in our lives. Some of us can testify that when Jesus begins to play on the keys of our lives, what a difference he makes. He teaches our hearts a new song of joy. He teaches our hands a new quality of service. He teaches our feet new directions. He teaches our minds new thoughts of excellence. Don't stop him from playing on the keyboard of your life today.

As the Life, Jesus brings not only excellence but also enablement. Note what comes immediately after he says, "I am the way, and the truth, and the life"—"No one comes to the Father except through me." That's why we can live excellently and abundantly, because Jesus ushers us into the very presence and power of God. In spite of our background and the sins we have committed and the mistakes we have made, we are enabled to come boldly before the mercy seat. That's the opportunity that Donald Trump's millions can't buy, that all the political power of the United Nations can't give, that all of the military might of armies, navies, and air forces can't compel, that all of the knowledge of all the universities in the world can't open. Only the excellence of Jesus can enable redeemed sinners such as us to be in the presence of the same power that lit the sun and hung the stars, and then to receive a touch from that same power to fuel our lives for whatever challenges lie ahead.

Jesus as the Life not only brings excellence and provides enablement in this life; he also grants eternity in the life to come. The wages we earn in this life of sin is death, "but the free gift of God is eternal life in Christ Jesus our Lord" (Romans 6:23). Who doesn't remember the great revelation of the gospel: "For God so loved the world that he gave his only Son, so that everyone who believes in him may not perish but may have eternal life" (John 3:16). Note the word *eternal* in both of these texts. God's children, whose lives have been made more excellent by Jesus and who have been enabled to stand in the divine presence, shall live eternally. When John Newton declared, "When we've been there ten thousand years, bright shining as the sun, we've no less days to sing God's praise than when we'd first begun," he was talking about eternity. When Charles A. Tindley declared, "By and by, when the morning comes, when the saints of God are gathered home," he was talking about eternity. When our ancestors sang, "When all God's children get together, what a time, what a time, what a time," they were talking about eternity. When we sing, "We shall behold him face to face," that's eternity. And Jesus, the Life, will usher us there.

✕✕ 13 ✕✕

The Word

John 1:14

And the word became flesh and lived among us,
and we have seen his glory, the glory
as of a father's only son,
full of grace and truth. (John 1:14)

TO UNDERSTAND HOW JESUS CAN BLESS OUR LIVES AS THE Word, we must understand how words were perceived by the writer of this biblical text. To first-century Jews, words were not simply sounds in the air; the word was a unit of energy and effective power. A word not only said things; it did things. Thus, when we read the account of Creation in Genesis, God speaks and things happen. Over and over again, we read, "And God said…." In response to what God said, light was created, water was gathered, earth was sculpted, stars were hung, birds soared, fish swam, animals roamed the land, and humankind was formed in the images of God. Thus the Word of God represents God in action.

Consequently, when we see Jesus as the Word, we are observing God in action. Jesus is more than a good man, a great teacher, or a powerful prophet. He is all that—and more. He is God in action. He is more than a supernatural being such as an archangel. He is God in action. All other living beings are created, but Jesus Christ as God Incarnate is the Creator who consented to human birth so that he could be one with us for a season, so that he could share our pain, know our temptation, encounter our problems, and then redeem us from our sins.

What distinguishes the actions of God from the actions of human beings is the durability of divine action. Humans build, but what we build decays in time. In the ancient world, humanity built great architectural and engineering marvels that were called the Seven Wonders of the World. But the Seven Wonders of the World built by human hands are no more. In contrast, the wonders created by God's hands are still with us to astound—stars that have never varied in their courses since time began; snow on towering mountain peaks that are closest to the sun while the valley floor far below is hot and dry; wind that blows where it wills, and we cannot tell from where it comes or where it goes; snowflakes that fall by the billions and yet no two are ever alike; a delicate ecosystem designed so that the carbon dioxide humans exhale is life for plants, which in turn give back oxygen so that we can live; sodium and chloride that by themselves are poisonous, but put together they make salt, which preserves and flavors our food; hydrogen and oxygen, which are both flammable, but combined they comprise water, which is used to extinguish fire.

The wonders of God are true, enduring wonders that time does not erode. Thus when we see the actions of Jesus as the divine Word, we behold that which endures the test of time. The blood from Calvary's cross has not been dried up, diluted, or washed away. It can still make the foulest clean, even after two thousand years. When the questions are asked, "What can wash away my sins? And what can make me whole again?" there is but one answer: "Nothing but the blood of Jesus." Somebody else declared: "The blood that Jesus shed for me way back on Calvary, the blood that gives me strength from day to day, it shall never lose its power."

That's why the power of Christ as the Word of God is always able to conquer the works of Satan. When God made human beings, we were created in God's image. Nothing Satan does can take that away from us. Satan can take away our health, our wealth, and if we allow him, our hope and our minds. However, we are still the creation of God, and the image of God is still present in us. All that we need is the right touch—like a buried seed awaiting the sunshine and the rain. No matter how far we have fallen or how long we have strayed, Jesus is able to awaken, restore, revive, resurrect, and recreate within us the image of God that sin has buried but not destroyed.

That's why we can't lose our salvation: because when Jesus as the Word, as God in action, does something, he does it for good. Once born, we cannot become unborn. We may cut our life short, but we cannot become unborn. A lamp that has been disconnected from its outlet is still electric. It has only been disconnected from its source. But, plug it in and it will give light again. A dress doesn't stop being a dress just because it's dirty; it just needs to be cleaned. If you're lost, all you need is a compass because the directional poles haven't changed. North is still north, south is still south; east will never be west, nor will west ever be east. Well, when Jesus saved us, he established the poles for our victory. One pole is called faith, another is called repentance, the third is called sanctification, and the fourth is called service. The devil may turn us around and mix us up, but he hasn't changed the poles Jesus established when he saved us. So when we're lost, if we pick up our compass—which is the Bible, the written Word of God—or call on Christ, who is the Word of God in action, the Word will put us back on the right track.

Jesus as the Word is God in action. However, words also communicate. So Jesus as the Word also has a message to communicate to you—a word that will act with divine power to transform your life, if you will allow it. If you're divorced like the woman at the well, Jesus is a word of restoration. If you've been caught in sin like the adulterous woman, Jesus is a word of forgiveness. If you're bound like Legion, Jesus is a word of deliverance. If you're in mourning like Mary and Martha, Jesus is a word of hope and resurrection. If you've given your all like the widow and her two mites, Jesus is a word of affirmation and support. If you're old like Nicodemus, Jesus is a word about a second birth. If you've denied him like Peter did, Jesus is a word about second chances. If you're young like the little boy with his noonday lunch, Jesus is a word about using what you have. If you're hung up to die like the thief on the cross or if you're up a tree like Zacchaeus, Jesus is a word of salvation. Whoever you are, Jesus who is God in action has a word for you. "And the Word became flesh and lived among us, and we have seen his glory, the glory as of a father's only son, full of grace and truth."

Yes, Jesus Christ as the Word is God in action, and do not miss the significance of where he acts—among us. Not only above us to judge us, but among us to give us joy. Not only above us to watch over us, but among us to walk with us. Not only above us to lift us, but among us to love us. Not only above us as the Holy One, but among us as our helper. Not only above us as Deity, but among us as deliverer. Not only above us as Lord, but among us as leader. Not only above us as righteous God, but among us as redeemer-friend. As Word, Jesus is God in action among us—wherever we may find ourselves. In sickness, he is among us. In loneliness, he is among us. In heartache and heartbreak, he is among us. In confusion, he is among us. In turmoil, he is among us. When enemies are on every hand, he is among us. Even when death comes, we are not alone; he is among us. "And we have seen his glory"—as the Word of compassion and companionship, as the Word of comfort and peace, as the Word of salvation and intercession, and as the Word of our sovereign Lord—in action.

✕✕ 14 ✕✕

Light in Darkness

John 1:5

*The light shines in the darkness,
and the darkness did not overcome it. (John 1:5)*

WHEN I WAS A FRESHMAN IN COLLEGE, I LEARNED HOW marvelous and powerful the human eye is. I learned that when it is operating at peak condition on a perfectly clear night, the human eye is sensitive and perceptive enough to see the light from a single candle some fifty miles away. When I heard this marvelous and almost unbelievable fact, I not only celebrated the marvelous capacity that God put within the human eye, I also understood in a new way what the psalmist meant who said, "I am fearfully and wonderfully made ... that I know very well" (Psalm 139:14). I was also awed to realize light is so powerful that an expression of it as small as a candle flame can penetrate fifty miles of darkness—not fifty feet or fifty yards but fifty miles of darkness. That means that, were there no obstructions, on a perfectly clear night, if someone lit a candle on top of the Empire State Building, we would be able to see it in Trenton, New Jersey. How marvelous the human eye is, yet we would not be able to see the candle flame if light weren't powerful enough to penetrate the darkness.

Some of us know about the power of light, about the power of *the* Light shining in darkness. We know this power because some of us haven't always been as close to the Lord as we are now. Whether we were fifty miles away, ten miles away, one mile away, or fifty feet away—the distance doesn't make any difference, because darkness is still darkness. Fifty feet of darkness can send a person to hell as quickly as fifty miles of darkness can. Pontius Pilate had many sins, not the least of which was agreeing to execute the Son of God; in contrast, the rich young ruler had kept all the commandments from his childhood and, according to Jesus himself, lacked only one thing. Yet both Pilate and the rich young ruler turned their backs on the truth and the Light who is Jesus. Herod was separated from Jesus by fifty miles of deep and dark sin, including the blood of John, Jesus' own cousin. Judas was separated from Jesus by only a few feet of darkness, for trading the bread of Jesus' friendship and for betrayal—"And it was night" (John 13:30). Both Herod and Judas lost their souls because they both refused to embrace the Light who is Jesus.

Darkness is darkness, but the Light is also Light, and darkness will never overcome it. Have you sometimes wondered why parents don't give up on their children, why some spouses continue to pray for their companions, why some of us persist in praying for people who seem to go from bad to worse?

Although folks may be fifty miles away from their Christian upbringing; fifty miles away from church; fifty miles away in a jungle of drugs, alcohol, lust, and gambling; fifty miles away in the ditch of depression or in the hog pen of denial—we know the Light can still reach those people. Jesus, the Light who shines in the darkness, can still reach them.

Don't give up on yourself if you're struggling with something that you can't seem to overcome. I know you've promised to give it up and you've tried to give it up over and over again. I know you've strayed for a while and before you know it, you're back in the same old mess doing the same old stuff again. But don't think that you're hopeless, because Jesus the Light is still shining for you. He can still reach you. Whether you're in ten feet of darkness or fifty miles of darkness, Jesus can still reach you. Maybe there are some obstructions in your way—the forest of other people and their influence or expectations, or the fog of painful memories you won't penetrate, or the towering mountain of your own ego, or the light pollution from the flashing strobe of the devil's lies—but still the Light who is Jesus shines for you. The problem is not with the Light, but with your obstructions. Perhaps your prayer ought to be "Lord, help me get past my obstructions so I may behold my opportunities. Help me get past the devil's lies so I might perceive your leading. Help me get past my ego so I might see your excellence. Help me get past my denial so I might see your deliverance. Help me get past myself so that I might see your message. Help me get past my blockage so that I might see your breakthrough." The Light is still shining for you.

Atmospheric, geographic, and architectural obstructions may obscure the light, but they don't stop it from shining. Or perhaps the bigger problem is that we have not turned our heads to perceive the light. Moses did not receive the message God had for his life until he turned aside to see the burning bush. Jesus as the Light has something for each of us if we will just turn to see him. Our testimony is that no matter how deep our darkness is, whenever our spirit is right, our heart is right, our motives and intentions are right, Jesus always has some light to brighten, to guide, to help us grow—some light that reveals what was hidden in the darkness.

Obstructions may obscure the Light. We cannot perceive the Light unless we have turned aside to bask in it. And we cannot see the light at all if we are facing in the wrong direction. If we are facing in the wrong direction, then we need to be converted, for *conversion* means to be turned around. Jesus told Peter, "Simon, Simon, listen! Satan has demanded to sift all of you like wheat (by obstructing your view and keeping you so distracted that you will not turn aside), but I have prayed for you that your own faith may not fail; and you, when once you have turned back [the King James says, 'when thou art converted'], strengthen your brothers" (Luke 22:31-32).

Therefore, if you are in darkness, don't think that you are hopeless. Just ask God to turn you around so that you can see the Light. Our prayer needs to be "Lord, turn me around." Education can help us analyze the darkness, and that's important—to understand the nature of darkness. But only the Holy Spirit can turn us to the Light. If, like Judas, we're in the illuminated company of saints but still in darkness, we need to pray, "Lord, turn me around." If all we can talk about is how it used to be, we need to pray, "Lord, turn me around." If we can't see Jesus for looking at other people, we need to pray, "Lord, turn me around." If a certain preacher has to be in the pulpit or a certain choir has to be singing before we see the Light, we need to pray, "Lord, turn me around."

The light shines in the darkness and the darkness cannot overcome it. Fifty miles of darkness cannot extinguish the flame of a single candle. That's truly marvelous. However, to really be blessed by the candlelight, we have to stand closer than miles away. To receive everything the light has to offer, we have to be so close we can touch it and hold it. If we are not receiving everything Jesus has to offer, perhaps we are standing too far away. We get closer only when we make a decision to draw closer.

I'm grateful that I'm closer than I used to be. Sometimes trouble draws me closer. Prayer draws me closer. My love for him draws me closer. And I want to get closer still, closer to the Light that shines in darkness. There's power in closeness. There's victory in closeness. There's warmth and comfort in closeness. There's guidance in closeness. So I echo the words of the songwriter, Fanny Crosby:

> *Thou my everlasting portion,*
> *More than friend or life to me;*
> *All along my pilgrim journey,*
> *Savior, let me walk with thee.*
> *Close to thee, close to thee, …*
> *Savior, let me walk with thee.*

Mighty Prophet

Luke 24:19

*"...Jesus of Nazareth, who was
a prophet mighty in deed and word before
God and all the people." (Luke 24:19)*

PROPHET WAS ONE OF THE MORE POPULAR TITLES GIVEN
to Jesus in his day. After the son of the widow of Nain was
raised, people proclaimed. "A great prophet has risen among
us!" (Luke 7:16). When Herod heard about Jesus, he
thought Jesus was John the Baptist or one of the ancient
prophets who had returned to life (see Mark 6:14-15 and
Luke 9:7-8). When Jesus asked, "Who do people say that the
Son of Man is?" the disciples answered, "Some say John the
Baptist, but others Elijah, and still others Jeremiah or one of
the prophets" (Matthew 16:14). During the triumphal entry,
when the crowd asked, "Who is this?" the answer was given,
"This is the prophet Jesus from Nazareth in Galilee"
(Matthew 21:11).

Jesus himself was comfortable with the title of prophet. When he was rejected at Nazareth, he said, "Truly I tell you, no prophet is accepted in the prophet's hometown" (Luke 4:24). When supporters warned him to stay away from Jerusalem, Jesus replied, "It is impossible for a prophet to be killed outside of Jerusalem" (Luke 13:33).

Consequently we are not surprised to hear the disciples during the Emmaus walk refer to Jesus as "a prophet mighty in deed and word before God and all the people." Note the description of Jesus as Mighty Prophet. Sometimes to our detriment, we emphasize the meek and humble, lamb-led-to-slaughter, turn-the-other-cheek side of Jesus, and we forget how mighty he is. We wouldn't be so quick to panic or talk about what we can't do, or to quit or throw up our hands in disgust, or to take matters into our own hands, if we remembered how truly mighty Jesus is.

The words *mighty* and *prophet* go together. Prophets are mighty because their power comes from a mighty God. One has to be mighty to stand before people, let alone to withstand the devil. As Mighty Prophet, Jesus stands squarely within the biblical tradition of prophecy. Whether we are talking about Moses confronting Pharaoh, or Samuel dealing with Saul or Nathan with David, or Elijah standing before Ahab and Jezebel, or Deborah directing the army of Israel against Sisera, or Isaiah telling Hezekiah to get his house in order, or Jeremiah opposing Zedekiah—we are talking about men and women of power and might.

Thus, everything we say about Jesus is appropriately introduced by the word *mighty*. He is mighty in friendship because he is a friend who sticks closer than a brother or sister (Proverbs 18:24). He is mighty in love, for "No one has greater love than this, to lay down one's life for one's friends" (John 15:13). He is mighty in salvation because he saves "to the uttermost" (Hebrews 7:25, KJV). He is mighty in his promises because he assures us, "Heaven and earth will pass away, but my words will not pass away" (Matthew 24:35). He is mighty in his presence because he is with us always, even to the end of the age (Matthew 28:20). He is mighty in his authority because the winds and waves obey his will (Mark 4:41). He is mighty in his forgiveness, even for those who crucified him: "Father, forgive them; for they do not know what they are doing" (Luke 23:34). He is mighty in prayer, so mighty that when he prayed on a mountain, Moses and Elijah stepped through centuries of times to talk with him (see Matthew 17:1-3)), and when he prayed over a boy's lunch, more than five thousand persons were fed (see Mark 6:38-44). And when he prayed outside of Lazarus's tomb, death's sleep had to release Lazarus to answer Jesus' summons (John 11:41-44).

Thus, as Prophet, Jesus is someone mighty on our side. We may not be much, we may not have much, we may not look like much, we may not know very much, we may not be able to do very much in and of ourselves—but we have someone mighty on our side.

As Prophet Jesus is not only mighty in who he is and what he does; he is also mighty in what he says. The prophets were those who brought God's Word to the people. Not their opinions or impressions, but God's Word. Not their prejudices or preferences, but God's Word. Sometimes it was a word that comforted, and sometimes it was a word that cut. Sometimes it was a word of judgment, and sometimes it was a word of joy. Sometimes it hurt and sometimes it healed. But it was always heaven's word for human need.

Jesus as Mighty Prophet brings God's word for our situation, whatever it is. He is Elijah's still, small voice in troubled times. He is Jeremiah's balm in Gilead for the sin-sick soul. He is Ezekiel's new life for dry bones. He is Daniel's lion tamer. He is Amos's mighty flood of righteousness. He is Hosea's longsuffering love. He is Habakkuk's prayer turner. He is Micah's steadfast love. He is Joel's outpouring of spirit on all flesh. He is Micah's willingness to stand alone. He is Malachi's tithe and total offering—a ransom for many. He is the mercy that Jonah failed to show. He is Haggai's judgment upon the nations and Nahum's passion for the city. He is Zephaniah's restoration and Zechariah's revelation. He is Isaiah's Wonderful Counselor, Mighty God, Everlasting Father, and Prince of Peace.

As a prophet mighty in word, Jesus is God's word—living, incarnate, active, revealing and fulfilling in our situation. Prophets of old declared a mighty word that said, "Thus says the Lord." But Jesus is a mighty word who says, "I am the Lord." Lord over sickness, sorrow, disease, self-pity, drugs, demons, and death.

Jesus is a prophet not only mighty in words, but mighty in deeds. The prophets of old preached repentance for the old life; Jesus brings redemption of the new birth—he is mighty in deed. Prophets of old preached forgiveness; Jesus *brings* forgiveness—he is mighty in deed. Prophets of old preached transformation; Jesus *brings* transformation (2 Corinthians 5:17)—he is mighty in deed. Ancient prophets died because of sin; Jesus died to redeem from sin—he is mighty in deed. Once dead the ancient prophets remained dead; Jesus rose to stoop no more—he is mighty in deed. Once the ancient prophets died, their disciples never saw them again; but Jesus is coming back again—he is mighty indeed.

Thus, as a prophet, Jesus is without peer. That's what Jesus means as Mighty Prophet. He is someone without peer or equal. There are many prophets, past and present, but only one Jesus Christ—mighty on our side, mighty in word, mighty in deed—yesterday, today, and forever.

✕✕ **16** ✕✕

King

Mark 1:14-15

*Now after John was arrested,
Jesus came to Galilee, proclaiming
the good news of God, and saying,
"The time is fulfilled, and the kingdom of God
has come near; repent, and believe in
the good news." (Mark 1:14-15)*

THE TITLE OF KING IS APPROPRIATE FOR JESUS BECAUSE the central concept of the Master's message was the coming kingdom of God. According to the Gospels, Jesus began his ministry with the message, "The time is fulfilled, and the kingdom of God has come near; repent, and believe in the good news" (Mark 1:15). And naturally, there can be no kingdom without a king. However, as we all know from history, having a king is not necessarily good news. When the people of Israel requested a king other than God, the prophet Samuel reminded them of the downside of having a king:

These will be the ways of the king who will reign over you: he will take your sons and appoint them to his chariots and to be his horsemen, and to run before his chariots ... He will take your daughters to be perfumers and cooks and bakers.... He will take one-tenth of your flocks, and you shall be his slaves. And in that day you will cry out because of your king, whom you have chosen for yourselves... (1 Samuel 8:11-18).

The nature of kings is to rule, and that's why so many of us are in trouble: we have the wrong rulers over our lives. Whenever we have the wrong rulers, that's bad news. However, Jesus as King and Ruler is good news because he redefines and transforms the concept of sovereignty. He is a different kind of king. Other kings desire more of the world—more land to consume, more wealth to control, more people to enslave. Behold what our King says: "My kingdom is not from this world" (John 18:36a). In other words, King Jesus says, "You can conquer all the land you desire, but you will not have touched my kingdom, for it goes beyond land. For my kingdom is not a kingdom in time and place. You can't find it on a map. My kingdom is a realm of existence; it is the reign of God that brings new birth and transformed being." To the critics and skeptics, Jesus declared, "If I cast out devils by the Spirit of God, then the kingdom of God is come unto you" (Matthew 12:28, KJV).

The kingdom of God cannot be located in any one place, as it is found everywhere. Wherever and whenever the lives of men and women have been transformed by the power of God, that's where the kingdom of God is and that's when it happens. Wherever and whenever people confess Jesus Christ as Lord and call upon his name, that's where the kingdom of God is and that's when it happens. Wherever and whenever the Holy Spirit takes charge of people's lives, that's where the kingdom of God is and that's when it happens. Wherever and whenever people bury old grudges, wherever and whenever people forgive each other and begin to live in peace and harmony with one another, that's where the kingdom of God is and that's when it happens. Wherever and whenever we do justice, love mercy, and walk humbly with our God, that's where the kingdom of God is and that's when it happens. For God's kingdom is not one of land but of the changed lives of those men and women whose strength has been renewed and whose minds have been transformed and who are seeking to discover in their own lives the good and acceptable and perfect will of God. That's what God's kingdom is all about, so it is nowhere in particular; it is everywhere where men and women call upon the name of the Lord and are saved.

As King, Jesus is one among us. So many times the kings and rulers of this world are removed and distant from the people. When they come in our presence, they are so heavily guarded and surrounded by so much security that we can't get near them. Many times the kings and rulers of this world live so isolated from their subjects that they cannot relate to common people and do not know about or understand our problems. But I'm so glad that we have a King whose name is Emmanuel and who is God with us. King Jesus understands, and he knows all about us. He is with us—in our pain, our sickness, our suffering, our temptation, our struggles, our trials, our failings, our disappointments, and our setbacks. I know he's with us because every now and then we can feel his power in our lives. Every now and then, we can feel his spirit burning on the altars of our hearts.

As King, Jesus is among us and he is also *for* us. For our sakes he left the glory above and became flesh. For us, he was beaten and mocked. He bore that cross up Calvary's brow. He suffered, bled, and died. However, to truly understand how radically different Jesus as King is and why his kingship is such good news, let us look at him in contrast to one of the great kings of human history.

Alexander the Great was a mighty king who lived three-and-a-half centuries before Jesus and who conquered the known world to create a colossal empire. Like Jesus, Alexander began his career at an early age, and like Jesus he died at the untimely age of thirty-three. But let's take a look at Alexander, and then let's behold our King. Alexander was born in a mansion; Jesus, in a stable. Alexander was the son of a king; Jesus was the son of a carpenter. Alexander died as a revered king on a throne; Jesus died as a mocked king on a cross. Alexander shed the blood of millions for his own gain; Jesus shed his own blood for the salvation of millions. Alexander died in Babylon in splendor; Jesus died on Calvary in shame. Alexander conquered every throne; Jesus conquered every grave. Alexander enslaved all people; Jesus set all people free. Alexander made history; Jesus transformed history. Alexander was victorious in life but defeated in death, for when they buried him, he stayed buried. In contrast, although it might appear that Jesus was defeated in life, he surely conquered death. Men buried him and sealed the tomb, but on morning of the third day, the women discovered the stone rolled away and an angel asking, "Why do you look for the living among the dead? He is not here, but has risen" (Luke 24:5). Although Alexander's power was great in life, when death claimed him he lost it all. But, when King Jesus rose victoriously from the grave, he could claim, "All power is given unto me in heaven and in earth" (Matthew 28:18, KJV). Jesus, our risen King, declares, "The power Alexander used to have—that's mine. The power that modern Caesars thinks they have—that's mine. The power that death and the grave once held—that's mine. The power of all rulers who have ever reigned or ever will reign—that's mine. The power of all armies that have ever marched or ever will march—that's mine. The power of all governments, past, present, and future—that's mine. The power of every nation, every kindred, and every tribe—that's mine. All power," declares King Jesus, "is mine."

Therefore, it is not the name of Alexander the Great, but of Jesus Christ, your king and my king, that God has highly exalted, "so that at the name of Jesus every knee should bend, in heaven and on earth and under the earth, and every tongue should confess that Jesus Christ is Lord, to the glory of God the Father" (Philippians 2:10-11).

All hail King Jesus, who is with us, within us, and sovereign over us and all creation!

✕✕ **17** ✕✕

Bishop of Your Soul

I Peter 2:25

Ye were as sheep going astray;
but are now returned unto the Shepherd and
Bishop of your souls. (1 Peter 2:25, KJV)

WHEN TRANSLATED INTO ENGLISH, THE GREEK WORD
episcopos means "bishop, presbyter (hence the term
Presbyterian), or elder." In the New Testament church, the
episcopos exercised a ministry of oversight, superinten-
dence, guardianship, and guidance of churches. Thus, when
the writer of 1 Peter in the King James Version refers to
Jesus as Shepherd and Bishop of our souls, he is saying a
number of things.

First, he is establishing that Jesus is our overseer. I don't
know about you, but I shudder to think where I would be if
I didn't have somebody looking out for me. When I think
about all the foolish chances I have taken and continue to
take—from dodging in and out of traffic in my car to dashing

in and out of trouble in my own wisdom rather than in God's Word and will—I shudder to think where I would be if I did not have somebody looking out for me.

When I was just starting to preach as a teenager, an older minister told me, "Remember, young man, there are enough holes for you to fall into naturally. You don't have to go looking for them." That truism applies to everybody, not just preachers! Between the holes that the devil will dig for you, and the ditches that other people will set for you for the sheer joy of seeing you fall, you don't have to go looking for trouble or sin. Trouble and sin will find you. When I think about the many times I could have fallen and the many traps that I escaped that I didn't even know were set for me at the time, I shudder to think where I would be if I didn't have an overseer, a guardian, looking out for me.

Now we should be clear about who our Overseer is. Some people talk about luck. There's not enough luck in the world to take some of us through what we have to go through on a daily basis. Some people talk about the stars. However, stars are created things governed by the rules of the universe. And when somebody who doesn't respect rules (or who makes up his or her own rules) is working on you, you need more than created things to watch over your particular case. We need Somebody who can overrule the somebodies who make up their own rules. Some people believe in the spirits of their ancestors. Well, I believe in the spirits of my ancestors, but I also believe in the One who oversees my ancestors. Some people have patron saints, but my Overseer sets the standards for the saints. Some people talk about guardian angels. That's all right, but why settle for less when you can have the best? My Overseer is the one who dispatches the angels.

Our Overseer, our Bishop, is none other than Jesus Christ, the eternal God who was manifested among us as the mighty one of God. His life was so righteous that the devil couldn't corrupt him, sin couldn't touch him, demons fled from him, sickness couldn't stand to be around him, death couldn't hold him, the grave couldn't keep him, and he now lives to watch over us.

As Bishop of our soul, Jesus is not only our Overseer; he is our Elder. As Elder he has been where we've been. That's how we know we can pray to him and that he understands—because he's been there. We know he understands our frustration when we can't get cooperation, because he's been there. He understands our disappointment with people who have no vision, because he's been there. He understands our tears when we've been hurt by those who love us, because he's been there. He understands our anger with petty, jealous, mean-spirited, vicious people (both in and outside of the church), because he's been there. He understands what it feels like to be talked about, lied on, and falsely accused, because he's been there. He understands when we feel deserted and lonely, because he's been there. He understands our dismay when we see enemies get a temporary victory and when we see demons gloat, because he's been there. But there's more: not only has our Elder been there; he has overcome. That's why Jesus is able to help us—because not only does he know what it feels like to be there, he also knows what it takes to be victorious from there.

As Bishop, Jesus is our Overseer and our Elder, but he is also our Shepherd. The writer of 1 Peter calls Jesus our Shepherd, and Jesus claimed that title for himself (see John 10:11). But, what does that mean to us today? Well, in the Christian church today, *pastor* is the modern ministry of the shepherd, and in the New Testament church, a bishop also was a pastor. The essence of a pastor is a caring heart. A great preacher in the pulpit is fine, but when the sermon is over, we need somebody with a caring heart. And Jesus is the quintessential Pastor.

Now, we must understand that unlike shepherds who often keep others' flocks and pastors who accept a salary for their labors, our Shepherd-Pastor, Jesus, is not a hireling. We don't come to worship or work in church because we're afraid that if we don't then something bad will happen. We don't tithe because we're trying to stay on God's good side. We worship, we serve, and we tithe because we're grateful for what the Lord has already done. Our Savior is not for hire. His cleansing blood is not for hire. His never-failing presence and ever-keeping power are not for hire. His promises and his Word are not for hire. Whatever Pastor Jesus does for us is because he cares. And whatever we do for him is only a response to his caring. Whatever we give is because he first gave to us. Whatever love we have for him is because he first loved us.

As Bishop of our souls, Jesus is our Overseer, our Elder, our Pastor, and finally he is our Sender. Bishops are known for their assigning or sending power. Bishops have to send other ministers to serve in various places. However, what makes me love Bishop Jesus all the more is that he's the only

Bishop who will send you and go with you at the same time. Whenever the Bishop sends you, the Bishop will also be there with you. And even if you find yourself in places where Jesus didn't send you, if you have embraced him in your heart, he will still be with you. Our Bishop didn't send Peter to jail, but Jesus was with him anyhow. Our Bishop didn't lock up Paul and Silas in prison, but Jesus was there anyhow. Our Bishop didn't send Stephen into the street to face a vicious crowd, but Jesus was there anyhow. Our Bishop didn't put John on Patmos, but Jesus was there anyhow. Our Bishop didn't send a prodigal to that hog pen, but if that prodigal calls on him, Jesus will be there anyhow. Our Bishop didn't send you to the unemployment line, but if you need him to make a way for you, Jesus will be there anyhow. Our Bishop didn't put you on that sick bed, but Jesus will be there anyhow. No matter where you find yourself, whether Bishop Jesus sent you there or not, the Bishop of your soul will be with you there.

Then, when you come to the end of your journey, that's when you make your greatest discovery about what our Bishop, Jesus, can do. For he is not just a bishop; he's the Bishop of your soul. And when you must leave this body behind, Jesus comes—the Overseer, Elder, and Pastor of your soul comes and carries you across death's chilly stream and brings it to a land fairer than day, where saints immortal reign.

✂ 18 ✂

The Great Amen

Revelation 3:14

*"The words of the Amen,
the faithful and true witness, the origin
of God's creation." (Revelation 3:14)*

THE AMEN? AT FIRST THIS SEEMS A STRANGE TITLE FOR
our Lord and Savior, Jesus Christ. We generally used the term
amen as an expression of praise and worship—and perhaps
that's exactly why it *is* such an appropriate title for Christ. For
a Christian, Jesus is the main reason for praise. What can
Jesus mean to you? He is the reason for praise. And why
should we want to praise God? Nothing drives the blues away
like praise. Nothing drives self pity away like praise. Nothing
encourages the spirit or lifts the heart or lightens the load or
puts sunshine in an otherwise dull and dim day like praise.

There are times in our lives when we just don't feel like
praising God. There are times when we are so down and out
of sorts that we just come to church and don't really know

why we're coming. We just feel the need to come. Our hope is that perhaps the preacher or somebody will say something or do something to help us get out of the mood we're in or to help us figure out our problems. Although we're in church and grateful and all of that, frankly praise is not in our spirit. The last thing we want to hear or see is some joyful and jubilant spirit telling us to stand up and praise the Lord. Sometimes we want to stand up and yell back, "Leave me alone. I don't feel like praising. I got all of these problems and I don't know where to begin to even start straightening them out. My love life is in the pits. My family is acting crazier every day. My financial situation is shaky, and these bills are about to suffocate me. I have questions about my career. I'm not feeling my best physically. I'm dealing with situations I didn't think I'd ever have to handle. I'm having trouble sleeping at night and praying at all. It seems as if the devil is waging an all-out war against me. And I haven't heard from God lately even though I have earnestly sought him. Frankly I don't have much of a praise spirit. I know I have my health and strength and food and shelter. I don't take that for granted. I am grateful, but with all of this other stuff draining energy from me, I'm angry, frustrated, uptight, stressed out, and I don't feel like praising."

It is precisely at those moments that Jesus the Amen can mean something to us. For when we look at Jesus, we take attention off ourselves. It is impossible to think about Jesus without thinking something good. And the moment we think about something good, we're on our way to praise. Whatever is said about Jesus will be something that elicits praise. No matter how bad we're feeling, if we hear the word *savior*, we realize that come what may from day to day "it is well with my soul." We know we have a reason for praise, Amen!

When we feel lonely and like nobody cares or understands and we hear the word *friend*, that by itself is powerful enough to bring praise. But when we complete the phrase "friend of sinners," then we realize we are loved when we are at our worst and we find ourselves, in spite of ourselves, saying, "Amen, thank you, Jesus." More than one sick person has been able to keep hope alive and renew a determination to recover just by hearing the word *healer*. More than one sick person for whom healing has not and will not come has been encouraged and more than one person weighed down in sorrow has been comforted when they have heard the expressions, "The grace of the Lord Jesus Christ be with you" and "My grace is sufficient for you." And their hearts responded with shouts of praise, "Amen! Praise you, Jesus."

No matter what we go through, what people put us through, what the devil sends upon us, the grace, the goodness, the blessings, the unmerited favor of the Lord Jesus Christ will be with us. That's enough to make us shout "Amen!" because we know that we have the victory. Some may wonder, "Why is that person doing all that shouting in the midst of all of these problems?" It is because that person knows that he (or she) has the victory. Jesus is the great Amen because he is what makes praise possible.

Jesus is the great Amen because of what the term means as well. *Amen* means "it is so," "so be it," "verily," or "truly."

In other words, *amen* is an expression of affirmation and confirmation. But what does *amen* confirm or affirm? The weather report? No, we don't "amen" that even when the forecaster is right. Some scientific discovery? No, as great as the scientists may be, they and their achievements don't merit such an exalted term. Some great legal decision? No, we may cheer a Supreme Court ruling, but we don't usually "amen" one. Some great political speech? No, we give the speaker applause, but not an amen. Some deep philosophical truth? We give assent, but not amen. Some popular tune? No, that would be casting pearls before swine.

Jesus as the great Amen affirms something greater than human words and actions. Paul, in 2 Corinthians 1:20, tells us what Jesus affirms: "For in him every one of God's promises is a 'Yes.' For this reason it is through him that we say the 'Amen,' to the glory of God." Jesus, the great Amen, is the confirmation of all the promises of God. How do we know that God's Word is true and that we can stake our lives upon it? Jesus who lived, walked, died, and rose among us is the great Amen. He is truly, truly the "verily, verily." He is the "it is so" and the "so be it" of God's promises.

In Exodus 3:14, God declared, "I AM WHO I AM." In John's Gospel, Jesus said, "Amen, I am the bread of life ... the light of the world ... the good shepherd ... the door ... the resurrection and life ... the way, truth, and life ... the true vine."

In Isaiah 43:1, God promised, "Do not fear, for I have redeemed you." In John 16:33, Jesus said, "Amen, in the world ye shall have tribulation: but be of good cheer; I have overcome the world" (KJV).

In Jeremiah 33:3, God promised, "Call to me and I will answer you." In Matthew 7:7, Jesus says "Amen. Ask, and it will be given you."

In Isaiah 55:6, God declared, "Seek the LORD while he may be found." In John 9:4, Jesus says, "Amen, we must work the works of him who sent me while it is day."

In Joshua 1:5, God promised, "I will not fail you or forsake you." In Matthew 28:20 (KJV), Jesus said, "Amen, I am with you always, even unto the end of the world."

In Malachi 3:10, God promised, "Bring the full tithe into the storehouse, … see if I will not open the windows of heaven for you and pour down for you an overflowing blessing." In Matthew 6:33, Jesus said, "Amen. Strive first for the kingdom of God and his righteousness, and all these things will be given to you as well."

In Psalm 16:10, "You do not give me up to Sheol, or let your faithful one see the Pit." In Revelation 1:17-18, Jesus Christ said, "Amen, I am the first and the last, and the living one. I was dead, and see, I am alive forever and ever; and I have the keys of Death and of Hades."

And if that's not reason to stand up and praise the Lord, I don't know what is! Amen? Amen!

✗✗ 19 ✗✗

Bright Morning Star

Revelation 22:16

*"I am the root and descendent of David,
the bright morning star."*
(Revelation 22:16b)

THE PHRASE BRIGHT MORNING STAR, LIKE LILY OF THE
valley, is one of the most culturally popular as well as most
theologically descriptive titles for Jesus in the African
American church. But why is Bright Morning Star such an
apt title or description for Jesus?

First, a star is something that we have to look up to see.
Jesus as Bright Morning Star reminds us that we ought to go
through life looking up. Many of us go through life looking
down. I'm always telling young African Americans (and
some older ones as well), "When you talk to others, quit
looking down as if you are ashamed or afraid to look people
in the eye." Don't you know that the eyes are the mirror of
the soul and that if you really want to establish yourself on

equal footing with someone, you should look at them in their eyes when you speak? So when we talk to somebody, we ought to think of Jesus, our star, and look up.

Some of us are not only inclined to look down physically, but philosophically as well. We're always inclined to see the negative—the worst—in life and in people. And some people have the nerve enough to identify that trashy or pessimistic view of the world as the black perspective, as if blackness excludes intelligence, beauty, nobility, excellence, class, honor, or that which is worthy of praise. Black people, quit looking down! Quit looking for the worst, quit slinging mud, quit reveling in gossip, rumor, and innuendo. Look up and fix your eyes on Jesus, our star.

There are those who are content just to look around—not down, not up, just around. They see things on their level. They see people and situations as they are, for good or for bad. Psychology, anthropology, biology, sociology, physiology, and other social and empirical scientific methods of study are fine for what they are; they see everything on one level— the human eye level. That is their limitation. Jesus as Bright Morning Star reminds us that sometimes, to get to the answers we are seeking, we have to elevate our vision above the human level and look up. The direction from sin to salvation is up. The direction from ignorance to intelligence is up. The direction from emptiness to empowerment is up. The direction from sadness to a smile is up. The direction from languishing to loving is up. The direction from jealousy to joy is up. The direction from trouble to testimony is up. The direction from helplessness to hope is up. The direction from despondency to deliverance is up. The direction from hell to heaven is up.

Jesus as Bright Morning Star is not only a reminder to keep looking up, but as a star he is represents that which no nation, race, gender, class, or church can keep to itself. We may hoard land, water, oil, minerals, grain, or food, but as a star, Jesus is not the private domain of anyone. Some people have tried to use Jesus as grounds for their sexism, but others (especially women) have seen in him an equalizer. Oppressors have used Jesus to justify their racist institutions and systems, but the oppressed have seen him as a liberator. The elite classes have used Jesus to guard their privilege, but the masses still see him as Lord and caretaker of the poor. Churches have used Jesus to preserve their dogmatism, but all believers still see in him a savior. The self-righteous have used Jesus to laud their narrow piety, but "whosoever will" still see in him a friend of sinners. No one can keep someone else from Jesus any more than one could lasso a star, contain the ocean, extinguish the sun, or keep the rain from falling. Jesus as our Star still says, "If you want to reach out and touch me, lift your voice and call my name. Pray to me in you inmost thoughts—I'm available to all but possessed by none."

But Jesus is not just any star. He is specifically the *Bright* Morning Star, the most brilliant of all other luminaries in the theological or religious sky. Only Jesus is a perfect combination of divinity and humanity. He walks beside us as companion and rises above us as conqueror. He is with us as a lover and above us as Lord. He is with us as a guide and above us as God. He is with us as inspirer and above us as intercessor. He is with us as Heaven's messenger and above us as heavenly mediator. He is with us as gospel and above us as grace. He is with us as friend and above us as forgiver. He is with us as helper and above us as hope. He is with us in trouble and above us as Trinity.

Of course, Jesus is not merely the brightest star in our sky. He is the Bright *Morning* Star, and as such he is the herald of the new day. We usually think of stars as nighttime luminaries, but the morning star announces the beginning of a new day. Who can testify that "since I met Jesus, it's a new day now"? I used to be bound by the devil, but since I met Jesus, it's a new day now. I used to have low self-esteem and was in a constant self-destruct mode, but since I met Jesus, it's a new day now. I've put down my blues guitar and picked up a tambourine of praise. It's a new day now. People and things that used to upset me don't bother me anymore. It's a new day now. Fear that used to paralyze me and guilt that used to beat me up have lost their hold upon me. It's a new day now. Glory, glory hallelujah since I laid my burden down—it's a new day now.

And so, we understand Jesus as Bright Morning Star as one to whom we can look up, as one who belongs to no person or institution or nation but who is available to all, as the light in our dark night sky, and as the herald of a new day. Let the new day dawn and let our faces be turned up to receive it—and to the One who ushers us into it!

✕ 20 ✕

Alpha and Omega

Revelation 22:12-13

*"I am the Alpha and the Omega,
the first and the last, the beginning
and the end." (Revelation 22:13)*

THE TITLE ALPHA AND OMEGA OCCURS THREE TIMES IN the Book of Revelation (1:8; 21:6; 22:13). In the first two instances, this title is claimed by God, and in the last reference the title is claimed by Jesus Christ. The fact that Jesus, the resurrected and exalted Christ, accepts the same title that is attributed to the Lord God Almighty is a reminder again of who Jesus is. Jesus Christ is God in human flesh. He is more than a good man and wise teacher, more than a miracle worker, a prophet, and a preacher. Jesus is God with us. Admittedly, I do not understand how the great God who made the heavens and the earth becomes a human being while remaining the God of the heavens. I do not understand *how* Jesus Christ is fully human and fully God. But I know it is true.

Many people are smarter than me, and they may understand many things that I do not. I do not understand how I can put a piece of paper in a machine called a fax and dial a telephone number, and then what is written on that piece of paper appears on another piece of paper in a machine on the other side of the world. I don't understand how so much information is stored in a small computer chip. I don't understand how I can turn on the television set in my home, just plug it into an outlet, and watch events in outer space. The explanation is simple for some people, but I have never been good in physics, technology, or mechanics. And yet because I use this equipment every day, I know that it is real and that it works.

Similarly, I cannot explain *how* people who believe in Jesus Christ as Lord and Savior call upon that name and experience victory over drugs, over alcohol, over enemies, over sin, over sickness—but I know that they do. I cannot explain how divine strength, perseverance, and renewal come from God to me—but I've received the gift of those qualities. I cannot explain how people become new creatures in Christ, but I have seen too many transformed lives to doubt the process. I have seen too many things happen (that ain't supposed to happen) for believers in Jesus to doubt the reality of what we believe. Only God's power can do what I have seen done in some people's lives.

So who is Jesus, the Alpha and Omega? He is God with us. I can't explain all the whys, hows, and wherefores, but I know that he is God with us. When I feel his presence in my life, I am feeling none other than the power of God. And when I'm laboring with problems and fighting the devil, I need more than the influence of a good man, the insights from a wise teacher, the bygone inspiration from a good sermon, or the memory of a mighty miracle. I need the power of God living, breathing, blessing, bestowing, working, producing, acting, and interceding on my behalf. I need Jesus Christ—God's very self, the Alpha and Omega, in my life.

Now, you may know that alpha and omega are the first and last letters of the Greek alphabet. So, Jesus as Alpha and Omega is at the beginning and at the end, and it goes without saying that he carries everything in between. Jesus Christ is sufficient for all that we need, from life's beginning to life's ending.

Nowadays we live in an age of specialization. People come to me for spiritual matters and go to lawyers for legal matters and to doctors for health issues, and even within those various fields there are further areas of specialization. However, the great joy about serving a savior who is the first and the last and who carries everything in between is that you just have to know the name. One name fits all! Jesus epitomizes one-stop shopping. For recovery from addictions, no matter what those addictions are—one name fits all. For release from guilt and fear—one name fits all. For reconciliation with family and friends—one name fits all. For healing from sickness or disease—one name fits all. For provision in financial crises—one name fits all. For comfort of hearts heavy with loss—one name fits all. For solving problems on the job or for resolving problems caused because we don't have a job—one name fits all: Jesus Christ, the Alpha and Omega, the beginning and the end, the first and the last, and everything in between.

To the young Jesus says, "Let the little children come to me" (Mark 10:14). To the middle-aged he says, "Come unto me all ye that labour" (Matthew 11:28, KJV). To the old he says, "In my Father's house there are many dwelling places" (John 14:2). To the young he says, "I come that [you] may have life and have it abundantly" (John 10:10). To the middle-aged he says, "My grace is sufficient for you" (2 Corinthians 12:9). To the old he says, "I am with you always, to the end of the age" (Matthew 28:20). To the young he says, "Ask, and it will be given you" (Matthew 7:7). To the middle-aged he says, "One does not live by bread alone" (Matthew 4:4). To the old he says, "Do not worry about your life" (Matthew 6:25). Jesus—he's the Alpha and Omega, beginning and end, and everything in between.

Jesus Christ, as the Alpha and Omega, identifies himself with God and incarnates God with us. He assures us that he is able to handle anything that comes between the beginning and end. And, finally, he reminds us of the place he ought to have in our lives. Jesus, the Alpha and Omega, ought to have first place in our hearts, first place in our minds, first place in our praise, first place in our living, first place in our loving, first place in our giving, first place in our priorities.

If we make him first, he will be our Alpha in all things—first to forgive us, first to believe in us, first to intercede for us, first to reward us, first to say "well done." And his promise is that if we make him our Alpha, he will also be our Omega. He will be the last to leave us, last to let us down, last to give up on us, last to condemn us, last to forsake us. He has our backs and our fronts, our past and our future, and in our present, he is God with us, now and to the end of the age.

✕✕ **21** ✕✕

Savior

2 Peter 3:18

*But grow in the grace and knowledge of
our Lord and Savior Jesus Christ. To him be
the glory both now and to the day of eternity.
Amen. (2 Peter 3:18)*

THE GREAT BIBLICAL SCHOLAR AND NEW TESTAMENT
commentator William Barclay said in his book *Jesus as They
Saw Him,* "No title of Jesus is more dear and precious to the
Christian than the title, Savior." This title describes the mis-
sion of Jesus coming into the world. When he was born,
angels told shepherds, "To you is born this day in the city of
David a Savior, who is the Messiah, the Lord" (Luke 2:11).
When he was grown, Jesus described himself by saying, "The
Son of Man came to seek out and to save the lost" (Luke
19:10). After his ascension back to God and glory, the early
church declared, "Christ Jesus came into the world to save
sinners" (1 Timothy 1:15).

Yet although Jesus is Savior, the times he is given that title in the Scriptures are not as numerous as we might imagine. In the Gospels of Matthew and Mark, the title *Savior* does not appear at all. It appears only once in Luke, once in John, and twice in Acts. In all of the Pauline epistles, it occurs only six times. It appears in neither the epistle of James nor of 1 Peter. It appears just once in 1 John. The title occurs with the greatest frequency—five times—in the short epistle of 2 Peter, which scholars believe to be the last of all canonical New Testament Scriptures to be written.

In fact, the number of times the title of *Savior* is attributed to Jesus increases in the chronologically later books of the New Testament. Evidently the early church had to grow to an understanding of what it means to know Jesus as Savior. Some things in life you only learn to fully appreciate in time. You can be taught *about* Jesus as *a* savior—that's head knowledge. You can *believe* Jesus to be the Savior—that's faith. You can *worship* Jesus as Savior—that's adoration. You can *meditate* on Jesus as your Savior—that's comfort. However, to really *know* him as Savior, that kind of certitude only comes by living and experience.

Some things about our faith can be learned from books, and we praise God for those valuable volumes. Some things can be learned from the testimonies and lives of others, and we praise God for that witness. But other things come only from experience, from maturity, from living, from wrestling with the principalities and powers, from coming up on the rough side of the mountain, from sleepless nights and tear-stained pillows.

Don't become upset if you know people who don't think

that they need a savior in their lives. Just tell them about the Savior you know, and let them keep on living. I'm glad I was taught about Jesus as Savior as a child, even though I didn't understand all that was being said. Because, later in my life when I discovered I needed a savior, I was glad I had been taught who my Savior was (and is) and that I could call on him with the certainty that he would hear me.

So keep on talking about Jesus as Savior. People may not pay you any mind now, but later on when the sin that is so pleasurable now becomes poison, when good times become bad times, when nothing they own can give peace to their spirits—they will know the need of a savior. And if they call on Jesus, they will know what it means to have *him* as Savior.

Having Jesus as Savior means that if you are lost, he's the way. If you're confused, he's the truth. And if your "get up and go" got up and went, he's the life. It means that if you're groping around in darkness, he's light. If you feel disconnected, he's the true vine. If you hunger for relationship, he's the bread of life. If your soul thirsts and nothing you have satisfies, he's living water. If you feel you have nothing much to live for, he's the resurrection. If you need protection and provision, he's the good shepherd. If you need opportunities, he's the door. If you're messed up, he's the second chance. If you're broken up, he's Mr. Fix-It. In Jesus, we have a Savior. Not a slogan, but a somebody; not a creed, but some company; not a law, but a life; not a philosophy, but a person; not a formula, but a friend.

As Savior, Jesus saves us *from* some things. He saves us from the sins that entangle by teaching us that through him we don't have to live in bondage. He saves us from ourselves by teaching us to focus on him as the center of our joy. He saves us from our foolishness, our wrong-headed and wrong-directed thinking, our backwardness, by imparting to us his wisdom and his vision. He saves us from the devil by teaching us that the power of evil is limited. He saves us from others by blessing us in spite of others. He doesn't save us *from* trouble, but he saves us in the midst of trouble by his presence, which helps us overcome trouble.

Jesus as Savior not only saves from; he saves *for*. People who are always talking about salvation in terms of what they don't do have an incomplete understanding of what it means to be saved. Jesus not only saves from sin; he saves for sanctification. He not only saves from hell; he saves for heaven. He not only saves from vice; he saves for virtue. He not only saves from damnation; he saves for development. He not only saves from envy; he saves for excellence. He not only saves from pride; he saves for power. He not only saves from lust; he saves for love. He not only saves from gluttony; he saves for greatness. He not only saves from greed; he saves for generosity. He not only saves from wickedness; he saves for wisdom. He not only saves from faults; he saves for faithfulness. He not only saves from can't; he saves for can. He not only saves us from ourselves; he saves us for himself. He's our Savior.

And as the songwriter Fanny Crosby wrote, "This is my story, this is my song, Praising my Savior all the day long; This is my story, this is my song, Praising my Savior all the day long." To him be the glory, both now and to the day of eternity. Amen!

✕✕ **22** ✕✕

Lord

2 Peter 3:18

*But grow in the grace and knowledge
of our Lord and Savior Jesus Christ.
To him be the glory both now and to the
day of eternity. Amen. (2 Peter 3:18)*

THE TROUBLE WITH THIS SERIES OF MEDITATIONS ABOUT
the names of Jesus is that its focus has been slightly one sided.
We have talked about what the names of Jesus can mean to
us without pointing out that, before and if Jesus is to mean
anything to us, something is required on our part. Before
Jesus can be the Gate, the Good Shepherd, the Resurrection
and the Life, the Great Amen, the Rose of Sharon, the Lily of
the Valley, the Bright Morning Star, the Alpha and Omega,
the Lion and the Lamb, the Bishop of our Souls—before
Jesus can be any of these things, something is required of us.

Our text tells us to "grow in the grace and knowledge of
our Lord and Savior Jesus Christ." Note that Jesus is not

only Savior, he is Lord. Note the order of the titles, not Savior and Lord, but "Lord and Savior." He is Lord before he is Savior. The lordship of Jesus Christ is primary and preeminent. In other words, before Jesus can save us, we have to do something first. We have to acknowledge him and accept him as our Lord. Before Jesus can save us, he has to be in charge. He has to be our reigning and ruling Lord because we are not saved on our terms, but on his terms.

That is not good news for some of us self-centered, "me generation" people. We want everything on our own terms. Not too long ago a popular song proclaimed, "I did it my way." Burger King has encouraged us, "Have it your way." I'm inclined to believe *that* is precisely what is wrong with a lot of our lives: we're doing things our way. Our marriages and relationships are exactly what we made of them because we have lived them our way. Some of us cannot keep a job and others of us are doing poorly in school because we are determined to do things our way. That is why some of us run from church to church, choir to choir, and can barely get along with any preacher—because we are determined to have our way.

Jesus as Lord is saying to us, "I am prepared to bless and build you, to save and sanctify you, to deliver and defend you, to teach and transform you, to fortify and fight for you, to heal and help you, to caress and care for you, but there can be but one cook in the kitchen, one chief in the tribe, one king on the throne, one president of the nation, one boss in the company, one lord of the manor, and that has to be me. You cannot serve the devil, yourself, and me like you have been trying to do. I must be Lord, and God must be God. After all, salvation is not given in your name, but mine. You were cleansed not with your own blood, but mine. You have authority over demons not in your name, but mine. You have access to the throne of grace not in your name, but mine. It's not your grace that's sufficient and your strength that's made perfect in weakness, but mine. If I am to be your Savior, I must first be your Lord."

There are no points to be negotiated in this voluntary takeover; no loopholes in this contract; no exceptions to the rules; no bargaining about the price. Jesus Christ is Lord. Salvation is a fixed-price item: it costs our submission to the lordship of Jesus Christ. Heaven has one entrance requirement: acceptance of the lordship of Jesus Christ. I repeat, before Jesus Christ can do anything for us, before he can mean anything to us, something is required of us. We have to receive him as Lord. But, what does *Lord* mean?

The "L" in *Lord* not only means love; it also means laws. Sometimes we get so caught up in talking about the love of Jesus that we forget that love has laws. The laws of love are truth, honesty, openness, respect, fidelity, commitment, courtesy, trust, responsibility, freedom, dependability, and understanding. Without laws love becomes lust, abuse, oppression, misuse, and exploitation. Jesus loves us but the laws of his love are determined by his lordship. For if we do not respect his lordship, we will misuse his love.

The "O" in *Lord* not only means opportunity; it also means order. There is a gospel song that we sing: "Order my steps in your word; teach me how to walk in your word."

Jesus establishes order in our lives. If we have disorder in our lives, Jesus didn't bring it. The person you're involved with may have brought it, but not Jesus. The "saints that ain't" may have brought it, but not Jesus. The Lord Jesus Christ is not the author of confusion. He establishes proper order. He says, "'You shall love the Lord your God with all your heart, and with all your soul, and with all your mind.' This is the greatest and first commandment. And a second is like it: 'You shall love your neighbor as yourself'" (Matthew 22:37-39). He says, "Strive first for the kingdom of God and his right-eousness" (Matthew 6:33).

The "R" in *Lord* not only means redemption; it also means righteousness. Jesus is a righteous redeemer, and he calls us to a life of righteousness. It may be old fashioned to say so, but God's people ought to be righteous. Not only fashionable, but righteous. Not only prosperous, but right-eous. Not only relevant, but righteous. Not only respectable, but righteous. Not *self*-righteous, but righteous. What is "righteous"? It is what Jesus Christ makes us when we are living by the laws of his love and when our lives are ordered by his will and his ways.

Finally, the "D" in *Lord* not only means delivered; it also means discipleship. We are disciples of Jesus Christ. We are not saved to go off and do our own thing; we are disciples of Jesus Christ. We are not saved to *lead* Jesus, but to follow him. As disciples, we have discipline, devotion, and dedica-tion to Jesus Christ. As disciples, we are converted, captured, committed, and consecrated to Jesus Christ. As disciples, we live, love, long, and look for Jesus Christ. As disciples, we are followers and faithful friends of Jesus Christ. As disciples, we work, worship, walk, witness, and are made worthy by Jesus Christ. As disciples, we experience, exalt, and expect Jesus Christ. As disciples, we are saved, satisfied, and sanctified in service to Jesus Christ.

Yes, when we do our part and receive him as Lord, then he who is Lord of wind and waves saves us from drowning in the storms of life, as he did for Simon Peter. He who is Lord of hell saves us from being tormented by demons, as he did for Legion. He who is Lord of forgiveness saves us from self rejection, as he did for the Samaritan woman at the well. He who is Lord of life saves us into eternity, as he did for a dying thief. "To him be the glory, both now and to the day of eternity. Amen."

✖ **23** ✖

The Christ

Matthew 16:13-16

And Simon Peter answered and said,
"Thou art the Christ, the Son of the living God."
(Matthew 16:16, KJV)

IN THE FOUR SHORT VERSES THAT MAKE UP THE PASSAGE
in Matthew 16:13-16 are found three of the most popular
titles of Jesus: Son of Man, the Christ, and Son of God. We are
accustomed to hearing Son of Man and Son of God as titles,
but sometimes we forget that Christ is also a title. Sometimes
we say "Jesus Christ" as if Christ were Jesus' last name. But it
is not, anymore than my name is "Reverend William Watley."
My *name* is William Watley; *Reverend* is my title. In the same
way, "The Christ" or "Christ" is a title, not a last name. What
are we saying when we refer to Jesus as Christ or Jesus the
Christ? I propose that we can mean at least three things.

First, the literal meaning of the Greek *Christ* (or *Messiah*
in Aramaic) is "the anointed one." Not simply "anointed,"

108

but "the anointed one." In other words, Jesus is someone whose life is anointed—drenched, saturated, filled—with the spirit and power of God in a special and unique way. He cannot be duplicated or replicated. In the Scriptures are many prophets, but there is only one Christ. There are many preachers, but one Christ. There are many teachers, but one Christ. Many leaders, but one Christ. Many miracle workers, but one Christ. Many healers, but one Christ. Many kings and lords, but one Christ. That's why Jesus is referred to as King of kings and Lord of lords. Consequently when we talk about the meaning of Jesus as Christ, we are talking about someone who chronicles, embodies, manifests, reveals, demonstrates, emulates, and encapsulates the spirit of God, Word of God, power of God in a unique way. Mohammed was a great prophet, but he was not Jesus Christ. Buddha was a great teacher, but he was not Jesus Christ. Moses was a great leader, but he was not Jesus Christ. The Dali Lama is a great presence, but he is not Jesus Christ. Only Jesus Christ is Savior. Only Jesus Christ is Redeemer. Only Jesus Christ lived above sin. Only Jesus Christ has conquered death, hell, and the grave. Only Jesus Christ is coming back again.

Jesus as Christ is the one in all of human history uniquely anointed and appointed to save. But not only is he the Anointed One of God; he is also Son of Man. This is the title that Jesus most often used in referring to himself. The title *Son of Man* occurs eighty-two times in the New Testament. With the exception of Acts 7:56, all the other occurrences are found in the Gospels. When the title is used in the Gospels, it is spoken from the lips of Jesus, with one exception found in

John 12:34. Why was this title so special that Jesus used it of himself eighty times?

I believe that when Jesus the Christ used the title *Son of Man,* he was establishing his identity *with* us. He is the Anointed One among us—not just among us, but the Anointed among us. That's why he could do so much while he lived on earth, because he was the Anointed among us. If we are going to make it in this world and work with people without them corrupting or distracting us, if we plan to battle life's problems without being broken, if we plan to handle the devil, then we're going to need an anointing—*you* need an anointing. If you're going to deal with Aunt Hagar's children, you need an anointing. You need more than education or sincerity or determination. More than one educated, knowledgeable, sincere, and strong person has been broken by life. You need an anointing—you need the baptism of the Holy Spirit. That's why Jesus told the disciples, "Before you go anywhere or do anything, stay in the city of Jerusalem until you are endowed with power" (see Luke 24:49).

But not only is Jesus Christ the Anointed One among us; he is anointed to serve. Whenever he healed somebody, he was serving. When he fed the five thousand, he was serving. When he raised the dead, he was serving. When he died on Calvary, he was serving.

I know that service is not a popular subject to the "me generation." We come to church for what we can get out of it. We think we are anointed to be self-righteous and to gloat and lord over somebody else. But religion is not about a shot in the arm on Wednesday, or a shout in the aisle on Sunday.

It's about serving the Lord and serving people. That's why believing is not enough and attendance is insufficient. We need to belong to a church and then become active in that church, because we serve the Lord through the organization and organism that he has established called *church*. God anoints us not because we are so special, but so that we can serve others in special ways. What have you done lately that is of service to God? Coming to church is not service. That's praise and worship, but that's not service. We go to praise and worship to be inspired to serve.

Lest we forget, service still counts much in the eyes of the One who is anointed among us to serve. He will still say to us when we stand before him, "Truly I tell you, just as you did it to one of the least of these … you did it to me" (Matthew 25:40).

Jesus the Christ is the Son of Man—not son of Joseph or son of the Jewish nation or son of black people or son of poor people only. He is the Anointed One among us for everybody. He still says, "Whosoever will let them come." I don't care how much we've messed up: "Whosoever will let them come." I don't care how old or how young we are: "Whosoever will let them come." I don't care whether we are male or female, black or white or brown or somewhere in between: "Whosoever will let them come." And whosoever will, I'm at your service.

But, Jesus the Christ is not only the Son of Man; he is also the Christ, the Son of God. As the Christ, he is the Anointed One. As the Son of Man, he is the Anointed One among us, but as the Christ, the Son of God, he is the Anointed One *who has risen above us.* But his example shows that to rise above, we have to serve below. It is by serving below that we reign above. It is by praying in Gethsemane below that we can intercede at the right hand of God above. It is by bearing a cross below that we can wear a crown above.

As the Christ, the Son of God, Jesus reminds us of our possibilities. Children of the dust though we are, mess-ups and sinners though we are, we have someone anointed among us who can lift us to our greatest potential. The mediocre become mighty. Sinners become saints. The addicts become achievers. The drunkards become delivered. The rejected become redeemed. The fearful become fighters. The ordinary become outstanding. The looked-over become looked-up-to. Children of sinful men and women become children of God. As the writer of 1 John says, "Beloved, we are God's children now; what we will be has not yet been revealed..." (1 John 3:2).

✕✕ **24** ✕✕

The Name of Names

Matthew 1:21

*"She will bear a son, and you are to
name him Jesus, for he will save his people
from their sins." (Matthew 1:21)*

FOR MOST OF US TODAY, NAMES ARE HARDLY MORE
than labels of identification. However, to the ancient
Hebrews, a name was more than a label. To the Hebrew
mind, a person's name was a serious matter because they
believed names told you something about a person's person-
ality and character. The Hebrews attached the same meaning
to a person's name as some of us today attach to a person's
zodiac sign. So when you told a Hebrew your name, you not
only told them who you were, you also told them what you
were. For the Hebrew, names meant nature. Because of this,
when a person's character changed he or she often received a
new name, which indicated a new being! Abram became
Abraham; Jacob became Israel; Simon became Peter; Saul

became Paul. And in the book of Revelation, Christ promised that anyone who overcomes will receive a new name.

The name Jesus, then, is more than a label of identification. It describes the Master's nature and the purpose of his life. It tells not only who he was; it also tells what he was about. The angel appeared to Joseph in a dream and said, "Do not be afraid to take Mary as your wife, for the child conceived in her is from the Holy Spirit. She will bear a son, and you are to name him Jesus, for he will save his people from their sins" (Matthew 1:20-21). The name Jesus is the Greek form of the Jewish name Joshua. And Joshua means, "The Lord is salvation." The significance of Jesus' name lies not in its uniqueness. Joshua was a common name in the Jewish community of that day, like Smith or Jones is in our culture today. The significance of the Master's name lies rather in its meaning: "The Lord is salvation." "You are to name him Jesus, for he will save his people from their sins."

When we hear the name Joshua, we usually think of the Joshua of the Old Testament. This Joshua was the successor to Moses. He attempted to finish the work that Moses started. It was Joshua who led the children of Israel across the Jordan River and into the land of promise. Jesus, our Joshua of the New Testament, was not the successor of Moses, but he was the fulfillment of all that Moses taught. Jesus said, "Do not think that I have come to abolish the law or the prophets; I have come not to abolish, but to fulfill" (Matthew 5:17).

The Mosaic Law sought to make a person righteous. As Christians we have that necessary righteousness, but it is righteousness based not upon ourselves or upon the law. Our righteousness comes to us because of our belief in Christ—in the sufficiency of his sacrifice on Calvary, which covers us, redeems us, and delivers us from the penalty of our sins. It is a righteousness that comes as God's gift to us based upon our faith in the one whose name means salvation. "Therefore, since we are justified by faith, we have peace with God through our Lord Jesus Christ" (Romans 5:1).

Jesus, our Joshua of the new covenant, picked up where Moses left off. He is the captain of our salvation. He leads humankind across Calvary and into the kingdom of God. Joshua's victory at Jericho opened the way for further conquest of Canaan. If he had been stopped at Jericho, he would have stopped indefinitely. If the power of Jesus' life had not been sufficient to deal with the weight and magnitude of sin and evil that Calvary represented, then the kingdom of heaven and the door to eternity would have been shut upon us indefinitely. But, since Jesus conquered sin on Calvary, he was able to go on and conquer death by this resurrection. And the walls that our sins, with Satan's help, had erected, which blocked off our entrance into eternal life, came tumbling down. Jesus, our Joshua, leads us not only in the conquest of the power of evil, but also in triumph over death and the grave. And we echo Paul who said, "Death has been swallowed up in victory. Where, O death, is your victory? Where, O death, is your sting? The sting of death is sin, and the power of sin is the law. But thanks be to God, who gives us the victory through our Lord Jesus Christ" (1 Corinthians 15:54-57).

The person of Jesus Christ, the power of this life, and the importance of his victory, epitomize perfectly the meaning of his name: "The Lord is salvation." Jesus, in fact, did what Moses tried to do—save God's people. Jesus' victory far outdistanced the conquest of the Joshua of the Old Testament. The apostle Paul tells us that "God also highly exalted him and gave him the name that is above every name, so that at the name of Jesus every knee should bend, in heaven and on earth and under the earth, and every tongue should confess that Jesus Christ is Lord, to the glory of God the Father" (Philippians 2:9-11).

It is said that a certain group of orange growers in California paid $2.25 million for the exclusive rights to use the name of "Sunkist" for their oranges (rather than also using it for prunes, raisins, etc.). That's an awful lot to pay for one name. But I know a name that is worth even more than that. Jesus himself asked, "What will it profit them to gain the whole world and forfeit their life? Indeed, what can they give in return for their life?" To determine the value of this name, you would have to determine that value of every soul that ever lived, every soul that is living now, and every soul that is yet to be born. For it is by this name and through this name that all people who have ever lived, all people who are living now, and all people who are still to be born, find salvation. Peter declared, "There is salvation in no one else, for there is no other name under heaven given among mortals by which we must be saved" (Acts 4:12).

Not only is Jesus' name priceless, but everybody can afford to use it. If you're rich, you can call on it. If you're poor, you can call on it. And it costs the same to call on it today as it cost more than two thousand years ago. Its price didn't go down in the depression of the 1930s and it hasn't gone up with the inflation of the last few years. A little faith is all you need to have to be able to call on it. The prescription is still the same: "Everyone who calls on the name of the Lord shall be saved" (Acts 2:21).

With car insurance and health insurance, if you have to use them, the next year the premium goes up. But the cost of calling on the name of Jesus doesn't go up when it is used. It costs the sinner what it costs the saint—just a little faith. If you get sick or get into trouble this year and have to use it, next year the premium is the same—just a little faith. You can't buy this name. You can't buy the power this name gives. You can't buy the victory that is won through this name. You can't buy the hope found in this name. You can't buy the salvation, healing, forgiveness found in this name. If you want what the name brings you, don't try to buy it; you just ask for it. Jesus promised, "If you abide in me, and my words abide in you, ask for whatever you wish, and it will be done for you" (John 15:7).

This name is priceless. And still it is affordable and accessible to all. But more than that, this name is always the same. My grandmother called on it. My father called on it, and my mother calls on it. I call on it, and when my children and my children's children and my children's children's children need a Savior, then they'll call on that same name, too. And no matter who you are or where you've been, you've got as much right as anybody else to call upon the same name they do. That Name of names is Jesus. If you let him, he'll be the same to you as he is to anyone else.